IF A STORE
COULD TALK...

The Spiegler Family Remembers

Allan Spiegler

ELDERBERRY PRESS

OAKLAND

Copyright © 2019 Allan Spiegler

All rights reserved.

Elderberry Press

1393 Old Homestead Dr.

Oakland, OR 97462

Tel: 541.459.6043

email: editor@elderberrypress.com

elderberrypress.com

Our books are available from all major booksellers.

Library of Congress Cataloging-in-Publication Data:

ISBN: 978-1-934956-75-5

If a Store Could Talk...

Subtitle: The Spiegler Family Remembers

1. American History—non-fiction.

2. Illinois State History—non-fiction.

3. Des Plaines, Illinois History—non-fiction.

4. Family Business—non-fiction.

I. Title

Table of Contents

Preface iv

The Beginning.. 8

Early Years at the Store... 14

Minnie, The Woman of the Hour..21

The Three Brothers...27

The Great Depression and World War II...52

Mabel and the Busse Connection...60

The Third Generation and Post-War Era 73

The Family Cottage 93

Comments from the Peanut Gallery:

The Fourth Generation 104

The Des Plaines Mall 131

PREFACE

This book began in 2010 when my parents, Roger and Elaine, decided to move from their house to an apartment in a retirement community due to health reasons. My mother knew that some major down-sizing was necessary and she asked me to take all of the family memorabilia she had collected for the past sixty years. Most of the material revolved around Spiegler's Department Store which the four generations of the family had operated for ninety years.

There were several boxes which contained newspapers, photo albums, separate photos, letters, books, pamphlets and WWII memorabilia. Even though I really did not want all of this material, as her eldest son, I dutifully took the boxes and shipped them to our house in Maryland, where they sat under the bed in the spare bedroom. I did not know what to do with this unexpected "gift" and at times thought of taking it outside on our gravel driveway and putting a match to it. No one would ever know or care. But my sense of responsibility to my parents and extended family would not let me do this and I knew there was enough material and photos to tell a good story.

This store began as a general store established by Louis and Minnie Spiegler in 1900 in the village of Des Plaines and over time was taken over by their three sons and later their grandsons joined in the enterprise. Although there were no heroes or saints among them, being ordinary people, as a group they served thousands of people in the area of Des Plaines by providing the necessities and comforts of life and participating fully in business, civic, social and religious organizations. Their ties with people in the community were remarkable, what they accomplished was considerable, and I felt this book would be a way of remembering and honoring them. They certainly deserved this.

I also wanted some record of the store, the family and employees who worked there to exist for future generations. Our children and grandchildren have no direct experience of the venture and people who worked there and only occasionally hear vague references to it. Some of them will want to know more of their roots and this will give them more of a sense of where and who they came from.

I have followed the suggestion of a friend in referring to national events which occurred during this time period also so that it would appeal to a broader audience than just family members. The comments and observations of older family members give some insights into what life was like in an earlier time.

In writing this book, I came to realize more fully that this store was not just a business where family members derived their livelihoods, but the psychological and social center of the family. It became who we were as people, and I imagine that many who participated in small family businesses and farms have a similar experience. I did not find the experience to be confining or burdensome. I feel blessed in having loved and been loved by family members and store employees, and in having warm relationships with customers and businessmen in the community. It has enriched my life immeasurably.

Finally, I would like to thank the Des Plaines History Center and the late Director Sherry Caine for providing me with additional photographs and a newspaper article. Those have helped provide a fuller picture of the store and the people who worked there. I would also like to thank Barbara Allen for the fine job she did of typing the manuscript and positioning the photos and captions, our friend Sidney Lemen for copyediting the manuscript, and my wife Fran for creating the genealogy chart and for technical assistance with the computer.

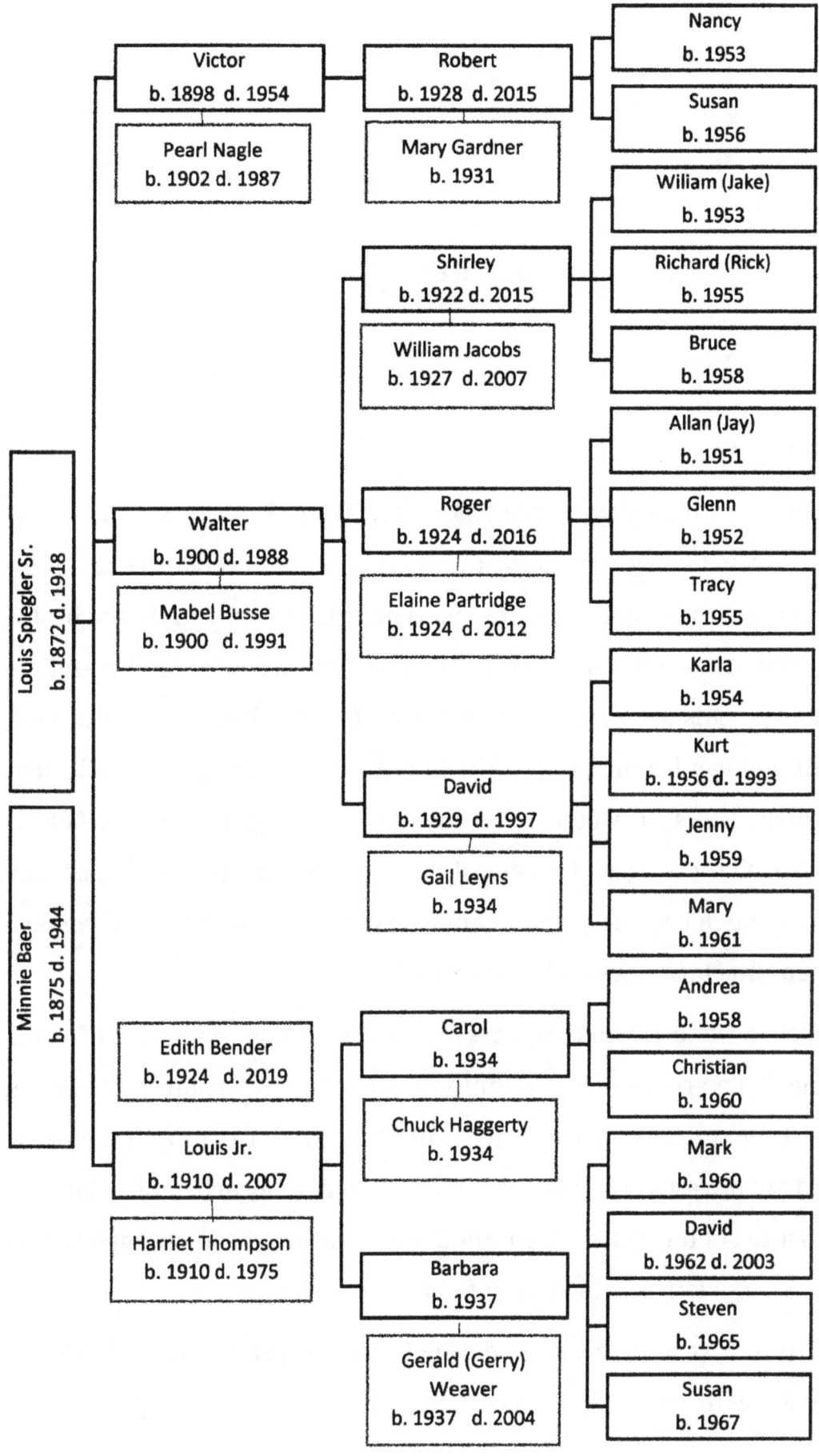

CHAPTER 1

THE BEGINNING

It was a winter day in late 1899 when Louis Spiegler sat in a train going northwest from Chicago on a hunting trip that he observed that the small village of Des Plaines could use a general merchandise store. His oldest brother had already begun a similar store in the nearby town of Bensenville and after the hunting trip Louis would discuss the prospects of the business venture with him and their younger brother, Benjamin. But 65 years before that notable day on the train, where Louis sat would have been virgin tall grass prairie. Before going forward to tell the story of the general store which Louis began in Des Plaines and the family which became a significant part of the community, it is worthwhile to go back in time to understand the beginnings.

French explorers and trappers had ventured from the colony of New France down the St. Lawrence River and into the Great Lakes region in the seventeenth century. They were amicably received by Native Americans and the Frenchmen travelled as far westward as the Des Plaines River valley in Illinois. They marveled at the vast sea of tall grass which stood over their heads and named the area Des Plaines or Aux Plaines, which meant simply, "the plains."

This tall grass prairie was a distinct geological environment which covered two thirds of the state of Illinois, much of Iowa and small parts of Indiana,

Missouri and Minnesota. It was a complex ecological community of about 200 types of plants and a variety of animals which included buffalo, elk, deer, bear and many smaller creatures. The dominant visual feature of this prairie were types of big blue stem grass and Indian grass which stood over a man's head. The thick vegetation and thatch covering the prairie burnt off during lightning strikes on a regular basis and left a soil of rich black humus.

Bands of Native Americans lived as nomadic hunter-gatherers on the prairie, the last group being the Potowatami Tribe which moved into the area about the time of the American Revolution. They hunted the game and fished in the Des Plaines River. In the winter they lived in wigwams built on a framework of tree saplings covered with mats woven of cattails and tree bark.

This natural environment had existed for thousands of years, but the lives of its inhabitants were to change radically and quickly with the advent of settlers from the east looking for good farmland. The Indian Relocation Act of 1830, enacted during the presidency of Andrew Jackson, mandated that all Native Americans living east of the Mississippi River be moved west of the river. The Fox and Sauk Tribes living in northern Illinois resisted and this led to the Black Hawk War in 1832 and their eventual defeat. The Potowatamis along with all other Native Americans were forcibly removed westward. Settlers began to trickle in at this point and Chicago was incorporated as a town in 1833.

Men from New England and New York who fought in the Black Hawk War brought news back to their communities of abundant flat land and rich soil. Some sought to leave the rocky soil of New England and by 1835 the Jefferson, Conant and Rand families were the first to settle in the Des Plaines River valley and begin farming. Other settlers were soon to follow, including many German immigrants from Europe.

The immigration of European settlers to the New World was an important part of the development of the newly-formed United States. From the period between 1840 and 1880 many people came from the British Isles and Western Europe to this country. Many came from Ireland due to the Great Potato Famine and others came from Germany due to frequent wars, social unrest, and a lack of available farmland. The 1880 census of the United States showed that of the 50-million Americans living in this country, 13%, or 7 million, were foreign-born.

With the great influx of settlers coming into the area and the plowing of virgin prairie into farmland, entrepreneurs felt that a railroad would be a profitable venture linking the northwest communities outside Chicago. The Wisconsin-Illinois Railway linked Chicago to Woodstock and began operation in 1854. Although the railway failed as a business venture due to the business panic of 1857, it was reformulated two years later as the Chicago and Northwestern Railway. The railway in Des Plaines and other communities northwest of Chicago was to form the site for the commercial hubs of these towns.

By the 1860s, a few businesses were beginning to spring up near the railway in Des Plaines. A livery stable, tavern and boarding house served the needs of the farmers and laborers in the area. Gradually a few dozen houses were built along planned streets and churches such as the First Congregational Church and Christ Evangelical Lutheran Church were erected. Des Plaines began to take on the "feel" of a town with a commercial center ringed by a residential neighborhood. When Louis Spiegler gazed at the village from his train car in 1899, there was a row of businesses lining Ellinwood Street. The street was dirt with planked sidewalks in places and the traffic was largely horses and wagons, but this forward-thinking man saw potential there and wanted to capitalize on what he saw.

When Louis returned from his hunting trip to his home in Chicago, he discussed the idea of opening a general merchandise store in Des Plaines with his brother Benjamin and wife Minnie. Louis and Minnie had married in 1896 and had a son named Victor who was born in September of 1898 and Minnie was pregnant with a second child. Minnie agreed to the venture and was to take an active role in the business when not busy with the rigors of raising small children.

Louis Spiegler Sr. ca 1897

Little is actually known about Louis Charles Spiegler and his family. Shirley Spiegler Jacobs, the family historian, states he was born on March 25, 1872 in the area of Schaumburg in western Cook County. His father was Barnabas Phillip Spiegler who was born in Germany and his mother was named Rosa. Louis had at least two brothers and at some point in time the family moved to Chicago.

Shirley states that the family had both German and Dutch roots. Roger, her brother, affirms this and states that a Dutch pronunciation existed with the Dutch spelling "Spieglar" of the name.

Minnie Baer Spiegler ca 1897

More is known about Minnie Spiegler due to a letter written to Shirley from Marie Baer, the daughter of Minnie's older brother Herman, dated June, 1988. Minnie's full maiden name was Wilhelmina Pauline Baer and she was born on May 10, 1875 in Germany. Roger states that she was born in the Black Forest region of Germany, which is in the southeast corner of the country. She had two older brothers, Oswald and Herman, two younger brothers, and a younger sister named Mary.

Minnie's father was named Nicassius Baer and he was thought to have been born about 1827 and to be some kind of structural engineer. His wife's maiden name was Melchior, but her first name is unknown.

Marie felt that the family immigrated to the United States in 1877 due to political tensions which had arisen between the newly-forming country of Germany and Napoleon III and France. The Franco-Prussian war had been fought in 1870 and France had to cede Alsace and Lorraine to Prussia. The family settled in Chicago and Mrs. Baer, apparently a strong personality, insisted that only English be spoken in the home and the family quickly assimilated into American culture. Nicassius lived to be close to ninety years old and dwelt in a cottage he had purchased in Chicago. Marie relates that he enjoyed visits by his grandchildren and would chat with them and insist that they drink a tiny glass of schnapps.

Nicassius was of the Roman Catholic faith, while his wife was Protestant. The parents did not push their children into either religion.

CHAPTER 2

Early Years at the Store

Louis and his brother Benjamin decided to form a business partnership to develop a general merchandise store in the village of Des Plaines and rented the vacant Meyers and Cumins building on Ellinwood Street. In the spring of 1900 the Louis Spieglers, including newborn Walter, moved to Des Plaines and began stocking the store with merchandise to prepare for opening. The store operated on the first floor of the building and the family occupied an apartment on the second floor.

The general merchandise store in a village or small town during this era operated much like the modern shopping mall of today. It supplied most things an individual or family would need to survive and lead a comfortable life, from clothing and shoes to furniture, from groceries to mops and brooms. According to the United States Census Bureau, Des Plaines had 1660 residents in 1900, and all of these people traded at the general store to get what they needed. Competition was minimal as the difficulties of traveling by horse and buggy on muddy roads kept people buying locally in their community.

In an original sales bill printed in October of 1905 the prices of many items sold at the store would seem amazingly low. Men's stockings sold for eight cents a pair; men's shoes for $1.60; brooms sold for twenty-five cents a piece; canned corn was fifty-nine cents a dozen and eggs were fifteen cents a dozen.

In the original cash expense book of Spiegler Brothers the following expenses were listed:

Suburban Times advertising:	$4.25
Store Rent	50.00
Six dozen eggs - wholesale	0.72
Horse shoeing	1.20

Salaries to employees were $5.00 to $12.00 a week.

The first year in business Louis and Benjamin each made a profit of $12.74. It takes a while for most new businesses to get off the ground.

In this enterprise, Louis Spiegler typified the entrepreneurial spirit and sense of optimism of the Progressive Era. Soon Henry Ford would be creating affordable cars in his assembly lines in Michigan; the Wright brothers would fly the first airplane at Kitty Hawk; Thomas Edison would invent the phonograph and lightbulb as urban areas gained electricity; and Alexander Bell would invent the telephone, all connecting people to each other and improving the quality of life. The process of industrialization increased, creating good jobs for many and men of great wealth such as Andrew Carnegie, John Rockefeller and J.P. Morgan. President Theodore Roosevelt embodied this spirit of optimism as he set aside millions of acres for National Parks, proposed a system of national health care, broke up monopolies which interfered with fair business competition and began the project of digging the Panama Canal. The United States was seen as the land of opportunity by millions of people, and the possibilities of financial success and leading a good life seemed limitless.

Fourth of July Parade, 1907

Benjamin sold his half of the partnership to Louis in 1904. Bob states that Benjamin moved to Naperville to begin a business selling field tile to drain soggy fields and marshes.

Roger relates the story that his grandfather Louis Sr. went to Chicago about 1910 to purchase a Stanley Steamer automobile. Stanley Steamers were powered by steam rather than an internal combustion engine and burned wood or coal as the fuel. Unfortunately, Louis was not very familiar with the automobile and unwittingly left the brake on all the way back to Des Plaines. The next day he had to drive back to Chicago to have the brakes fixed. Bob states that this may have been the first automobile in Des Plaines. Louis Sr. was very progressive in all that he did.

EARLY DAYS AT THE STORE

Interior of Store, 1908

This is a photograph of the interior of the store in its first decade. Most merchandise was laid on tables as opposed to being on clothing racks.

Louis was one of the founding Board of Directors of the First National Bank of Des Plaines. He was a very energetic man and a journalist observed that he was involved with most of the major developments of the village while owning the store.

Despite the press of managing a business and taking care of a family, Louis took the time to nourish the spiritual aspect of his life. He was a member of Christ Evangelical Lutheran Church and sang in the men's choir.

Minnie was a Roman Catholic. Roger states that Des Plaines only had a Catholic mission church without a permanent pastor in 1900 and thus Minnie decided to join the First Congregational Church. Her sons and their families all came to be members of this church. It is unclear whether Louis Sr. made the switch.

Fabric Dept. 1904. The lights hanging from ceiling were run on natural gas, as electric lights were not common.

Walter recalled that there was a hitching rail in front of the store where people could tether their horse and buggies when they came to shop. In the winter when snow was on the ground, the farmers would come into town to the store on horse-drawn sleighs. He also recalled that there were two taverns on Ellinwood Street, one owned by the family of his good friend, Dewey Imig.

The store was built on a platform which had wooden steps going up to the front door. In 1910 Louis decided to have the building lowered to street level and moved 22 feet to the west end of the lot. Later an addition was built which became the men's department. Louis can be seen standing in front of the building in the next photo. Louis Jr., their third son, was also born in September of 1910.

On January 13, 1914, at 1:00 a.m., a disastrous fire of unknown origin destroyed the entire building and merchandise inside. Walter states the family narrowly escaped being engulfed in flames and fortunately everyone was safe. The family moved to a new residence on Lee Street with what belongings they salvaged from the fire. Louis, undiscouraged, had the rubble cleared away and had a new, improved structure built made of steel girders and brick.

The family never resided in the building again. When the new store was built, the grocery section occupied the second floor. Progress and expansion were the ultimate fruit of the disaster.

In 1917 Louis suffered a serious stroke which left him partially incapacitated. Minnie had to resume the duties of managing the store along with the help of her two sons who were young adults. Louis never recovered from the stroke and Shirley states that at one point he was bled with leeches as the medical understanding of the nature of a stroke was poor in those days. As Louis declined, he asked his wife Minnie to sell the business which was heavily in debt. He felt that there was no way she could manage the business and the family by herself. Minnie continued to operate the business with the help of her sons during his long illness, however. Louis died in September of 1918 and he was buried in the Town of Maine cemetery where Minnie was to join him by his side when she died.

CHAPTER 3

Minnie, The Woman of the Hour

Minnie considered the words her dying husband had spoken to her about selling the business. It was true that running a business by herself would be a lot of work, and she had the welfare of eight-year-old Louis Jr. to consider. And the family was in debt due to the fire and rebuilding of the store. It would be a difficult nut to crack. Then there was the social issue. Women in the early twentieth century did not normally own businesses. They were not considered competent to do so. Although the suffragettes were marching in the streets, women could not even vote and Congress would not give women the right to vote until 1920.

On the other hand, Minnie had participated in the running of the store with her husband since 1900. Roger notes that Minnie had worked at Wieboldt's Department Store on Milwaukee Avenue in Chicago before her marriage, and thus had previous experience in retailing. She knew the wholesale suppliers and customers in the community. Victor and Walter were now young men, and would be available to help. And then there was always the question of how would she support the family and live if the store was sold? To sell the store and move to Chicago seemed like a step backward, rather than a step forward.

Ultimately Minnie made the decision to continue the business, and she did what was necessary to make it a success. The Great War was over, and the Roaring Twenties and better times were ahead. The business thrived and grew as Des Plaines thrived and grew.

Shirley reminisces about her grandmother in a paper she wrote for a communications course at Oakton Community College in 1975 entitled "My People." She states:

"The Women's Liberation Group would have called my paternal grandmother 'Sister.' In 1900, with two babies, she worked with my grandfather in their dry goods store. Ten years later, she had another son, but the interruption was slight. A housekeeper took care of the children, and Grandma 'worked.' The only homemade goodies her grandchildren received at her apartment were baked by the maid.

"A fire, rebuilding, and expansion placed my grandparents deeply in debt. Just before my grandfather died in 1918, he begged Grandma to sell the business. Instead, she took over and put it in the black. A 250-pound salesman once told me that the little lady was one of the 'shrewdest ever in the business.' She would have embraced the natural foods group. She preached the value of bran cereal, whole wheat bread, white meat of chicken, honey, figs, and fresh fruit and vegetables."

A paved Ellinwood Street, rebuilt store in foreground, ca 1919

Minnie: The Woman Of The Hour

Minnie continued to work long hours at the store until her death in 1944 at the age of 68. She was financial head of the company, buyer, and waited on customers. Gradually her sons assumed more of these responsibilities. From this vantage point she knew most of the people in the town and was well-liked and respected.

This building was built on Lee Street after the store burned down and the family occupied an apartment on the second floor. The building was near the back end of the store on Ellinwood Street and the old city hall and volunteer fire department were just north of it on the corner of these two streets. The Ziehn family deli and apartment occupied the first floor.

Minnie with Gertrude Ziehn in garden behind the store. ca 1928

Carol remembers that there was a long table in her grandmother's kitchen where the children gathered to have pie. She states her grandmother was tall and slender and wore simple house dresses and a net in her hair. She used to marvel how Minnie was able to put on those narrow high-laced black shoes she saw in the bedroom closet.

Bob, Victor's son, recalls that his grandmother was very efficient and frugal. Even though she owned a store which sold groceries, she raised a vegetable garden behind her apartment. She normally bought wholesale groceries for the store in bulk to save money. Bob remembers that when large sacks of sugar came into the store, a string was sewn on the upper seam of the bag which was removed to open the bag. Minnie would save that string and use it to wrap packages for mailing at the store.

Shirley notes that her grandmother was well thought of in the town. When Shirley was a little girl growing up in Des Plaines, she was always introduced to others in the community as "Mrs. Spiegler's granddaughter." It became a part of her persona, her identity, and gave others in the community a handle to know who she was.

Minnie with Shirley 1923

There were times when Shirley did not want to be identified so closely with her grandmother, however. In a letter to her nieces and nephews dated in 1989, she recalls humorously:

"I received a call from the Historical Society. They had a picture of the men's chorus, but it had no date. One of the singers was Grandpa Spiegler. The thing that interested me was that Grandma Spiegler had a terrible voice. When you stood next to her in church, you really had to concentrate on what you were singing because there was no resemblance between the tune and what you were hearing from her. If you were next to Dad (Walter), it was just as bad. He inherited not only her looks, but her voice."

Minnie was a great believer in the power of education. She encouraged Walter to attend high school and graduate at Thacker School even though many adolescents did not attend high school at that time and she could have used him in the store. Louis Jr. began attending Knox College in 1928 and graduated in 1932 even though the Depression was in full swing and money was tight.

Although busy in managing the store, Minnie took the time to participate in social and civic organizations. She was a member of the Eastern Star and the Arimatheus Shrine, Royal Neighbors, and the Social Union of the Congregational Church. For a long time she was active in the Women's Relief Corps, which did charitable work in the community. Her sons and grandchildren followed her example in being very active in fraternal and civic organizations which benefitted Des Plaines.

CHAPTER 4

THE THREE BROTHERS

*Three Spiegler brothers, (left to right)
Victor, Louis Jr., and Walter, ca 1950*

And so a general store which was begun by two brothers, Louis and Benjamin, came to be inherited by Louis and Minnie's three sons, Victor, Walter and Louis Jr. It would be a remarkable enough that a gutsy and intelligent woman born in Germany would successfully manage a business well into World War II, but the fact that her three sons were so dedicated to the business and the community for such a great length of time makes it even more remarkable. Their long tenure managing the department store meant it would have a major impact on Des Plaines in the twentieth century and be the economic and psychological center of the extended family during that time period.

The fact that all three of the brothers felt comfortable being merchants and did not peel off to another profession is unusual in the modern era, but less so in earlier times. Sons often followed in the footsteps of their father in their work, and the need to make a living and survive was more pressing, as there was no social net. The store was all the boys knew, as they lived in the apartment above it until the fire of 1914, and then in the apartment nearby. Having gone through the traumatic experience of escaping the fire and see all the family possessions burn, the rigors of rebuilding the store and the family being in debt, the long incapacitating illness of their father which ended in his death, and then the obvious need of their mother for their assistance in running the store must have roused a strong sense of allegiance to the store and the family as a whole. Only Walter ventured out to enlist in the Army after graduating in June of 1918, but World War I was over before he was called to serve and he remained working at the store.

Another remarkable aspect of the story is the length of time in which these three brothers were involved in the store and worked there. Victor, born in 1898, lived in the second floor apartment above the store as a toddler, worked as stock boy and delivery boy there as a teen, and eventually served as president and general manager of the store until his death in 1954. Walter worked there beginning as a teenager until he retired in 1986, a span of seventy years. He was to develop Alzheimer's disease and died two years later. Louis, Jr., born in 1910, retired at age seventy-eight after selling the business, and would have been involved with the store his whole life, but was blessed with extraordinary longevity and lived two decades after retiring, still mentally alert and chipper.

Each of the brothers was a unique personality with unique instincts and experiences. It would not do them justice to just lump them together as three merchants managing the family business. I would like to spend a few moments highlighting each one, telling stories from family members who knew them well.

Victor

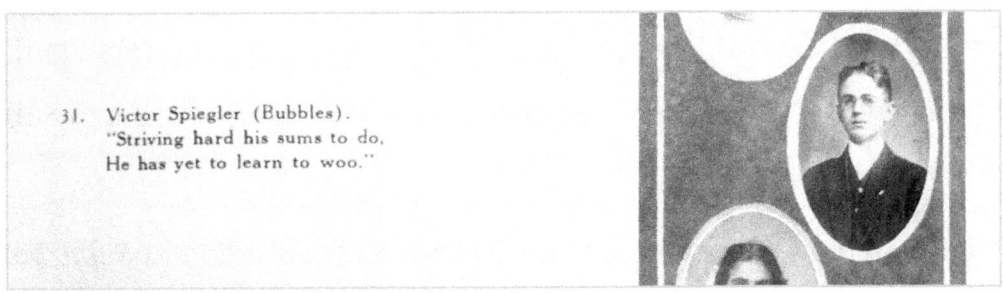

Victor, Maine High School year book, p. 23, 1915

Victor, known as "Vic," was a man of leadership capabilities who did not shy away from the limelight. He had boundless energy and goodwill towards others, both in his work at the store and serving the community. He did everything with confidence and fullness of intent; "half-hearted" was not a word in his vocabulary. Over time he became the general manager of the store and oversaw the finances as Minnie became older. He served as a fireman and secretary of the volunteer fire department for twenty-five years. It was not enough for Vic to be a fireman; he had to drive the fire truck.

Victor's niece Shirley made the following observations in her paper "My People."

"My world was peopled with relatives. Dad's eldest brother lived next door to us, and I grew up with two fathers. Victor was as excitable as Dad was calm, as dogmatic as my father was flexible and tractable, as loud as my father was soft-spoken. Victor did everything with the full expansion of his lungs. When he was angry, he bellowed; when he was happy, he roared; and when he was sad, he cried and the tears rolled from his crossed eyes unashamedly.

"He thought the town belonged to him, and he took care of it. In the days of the volunteer fire department, he drove the fire truck. He became upset by the number of accidents and deaths at a particular intersection, he stood at that intersection and physically counted the traffic to recommend some kind of control. He worked countless hours to interest organizations in cleaning up the banks of the river. When he died, I could see him in heaven, barking his advice to Saint Peter on how to run the place."

The following article which was printed in the *Des Plaines Suburban Times* in October of 1922 gives an interesting picture of Vic. He was a bit of a character, in the best sense of the word. Note the familiar style in which the article is written. Des Plaines was a town where people knew each other personally and could laugh with each other at certain situations.

Garage Burns As Vic Fiddles; 1000 Aces Go in Smoke

Another good feature for the week, along with the cowboy story about Chief of Police Christ Wegner, concerns the breaking up of a pinochle game just when Vic Spiegler, rated the best pinochle player in Des Plaines claims he was about to lay down 1000 aces and collect the bounty.

Plugging along with his usual slow start, which saw him somewhat in the red, Vic, who is also secretary of the fire department, was just ready to get even and count out his 1000 aces. Firemen members of the department, who had concluded their evening's business, were Vic's intended victims (say, there's a combination of words) in the 1000 bid.

This was all Tuesday night after the Firemen meeting which the boys wouldn't come to unless Chief Axel let them play pinochle after the evening's business was over.

But getting back to Vic. With the old victory gleam, Vic was all set for his bid when Police Chief Wegner, (yes he get's in this story too) poked his head in the fireroom yelling, 'Vic, your garage is on fire.'

Vic didn't like to lay down that hand but the boys were already on the way across the alley where Vic's garage was really burning, and right merrily. It didn't take long to get the flames under control but the fire had serious possibilities, back there in the Ellinwood business alley. Fire caused considerable damage and the boys had a job on their hands in getting it out. Vic's car and the Spiegler Store truck were slightly damaged but were yanked out before they were seriously burned. Spontaneous combustion was listed as the cause.

Vic himself had quite a time at his own fire, the boys report. Incidentally he is going to have a better time trying to prove he had those 1000 aces in that fire-interrupted hand.

Victor was married to Pearl Nagel in 1923, a year after Walter married Mabel Busse. In 1924 they built brick homes next to each other on Prairie Avenue at Laurel Avenue. They walked to work each day from home and their homes still stand today.

Homes of Walter and Victor on Prairie Avenue

Robert, the son of Victor and Pearl, generally known as "Bob," was born 1928.

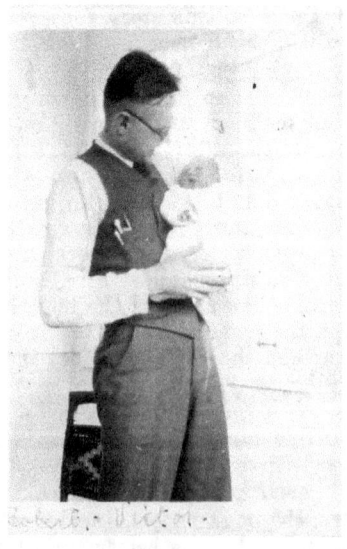

Victor holding newborn Bob, 1928.

In her paper Shirley recalls the following about her Uncle Victor after discovering that her grandfather Louis sang in the men's choir at Christ Lutheran Church.

"Then there was Victor. His voice was untrained, but it was good, GOOD, and he could harmonize beautifully with any song. He always led the singing at the Lions Club or any other civic group where there was singing. (A simpler time. We often sang for pleasure.) At least now I know that his voice had to have come from Grandpa."

Mary, who married Bob, recalls one of her father-in-law's habits with a smile. She said he always used to smoke cigars while working at the store. When he stopped to wait on a customer, he would put his lit cigar on a ledge or shelf so he could come back to it later. After waiting on the customer, however, he would often forget about his cigar, it would go out, and just sit there on the shelf. Mary said you could walk around the store and see cigar stubs here and there all over the place. It was a different era.

Although busy managing the store, heading his family and being a volunteer fireman, Victor took the time to be involved in church and civic organizations. He was a member of the First Congregational Church and a lifelong member of the Des Plaines Lions Club. He served as president of this organization one year. The Lions Club is more than a social organization and it serves the community in providing equipment to schools and helping needy families. Victor also served as President of the Chamber of Commerce, an organization meeting the business needs of the community.

One of Victor's passions was cleaning up the Des Plaines River which had become an eyesore in certain areas. Some people chose to dump trash and old appliances down the banks of the river. Victor worked hard to organize businesses and civic organizations to clean up the trash and keep the river beautiful and safe. Des Plaines named a small grassy area next to the river as Spiegler Park to commemorate Victor's efforts in this regard.

Commemorative plaque honoring Victor in Spiegler Park near river.

Close-up of plaque from Des Plaines Lions Club.

Walter

Victor, called the "family patriarch" by a journalist in an article written in 1950, died unexpectedly of complications following routine surgery on his colon in 1954. Walter, who had been managing the men's department for the past thirty years, was the next oldest of the brothers and the logical choice to receive the mantel of leadership. He was to carry this mantel well for over thirty years in guiding the company and the family.

Walter and Mabel Spiegler, 1922

Walter, as alluded to by his daughter Shirley, was a very different personality than Victor. He was a mild-mannered, unassuming man who I never observed being angry or even raising his voice. He was the master of the friendly smile and gentle answer. If there was a conflict or problem, his general perspective was that it could be worked out. He was not a person who naturally sought out positions of leadership, and so his style of running the company was different than Victor's.

The grocery department which was managed by Louis Jr. was closed in 1947 and Roger returned home from college to manage the Men's Department in 1949, so Walter and Louis took over managing the shipping and receiving tasks and spent the vast majority of their time at the rear end of the basement which backed up to the alley. Each day large boxes of merchandise delivered by trucks were slid down a long wooden ramp made slick through age and wear to the basement. Walter and Louis would methodically open each box and inspect and count the merchandise while comparing this to the original order forms of the buyers, Pearl, Bob, Roger, David, and Louis' son-in-law, Gerry Weaver. The merchandise was put on a large green marking table where ribbons of price tags were made by Helen Lewerenz, the venerable seamstress, on a machine cranked by hand. A stock boy then took the merchandise to the stockrooms or upstairs to be displayed and sold.

Although this was an essential and important function in the running of the store, it was not exactly what you would expect the president and vice-president of the company to be doing. An intelligent and dedicated person could be trained to do this in a month. There was a small executive office located on the second floor across from the business office. In this boardroom there was a long table, some chairs, and a large portrait of Louis, Sr. on the wall behind the table. But, in all the years I was in and out of the store and worked there, I never saw anyone in the room, although it was used occasionally by the salesmen to show new lines to the buyers. I never even saw the light on. In a way, the vacant office was symbolic of Walter's style of management. The office was empty because there was no need for an executive scrutinizing and controlling the operation, writing directives to underlings and giving orders to employees. Walter had found another way.

In Walter's style of management, he allowed the managers and employees a maximum amount of responsibility and freedom to do their jobs well. There was a general climate of good feelings, friendly relationships, and high morale which motivated staff to work at the store a long time and be dedicated to the store and their work. As the employees had worked at the store such a long time, for decades, they really knew their jobs well and were very competent.

It was rare I ever saw either Walter or Louis outside of the basement and up on the main floor. They never went around looking at displays and asking employees to make changes. The managers who were family did this. I never saw Walter order anyone to do anything, and it was rare he even asked anyone to do anything. Generally he would only ask the stock boy or us young family members to carry a box or move something around. His way was just to chat with employees, smile and joke as he came in the store in the morning, and occasionally he would sit with employees gathered around the luncheon table in the basement. The line between employee and friend was largely blurred in these relationships, and everyone liked him and held him in high esteem.

The only time Walter would appear on the showroom floor was at the end of the day, as the clerks were cashing out the day's receipts in the cash register. It was Walter's final task of the day to take all the cash and checks, put them in a leather pouch, and walk them down to the bank at the corner. As I look back on this now, I can see that the sense of safety and security must have been very high in Des Plaines in the 1950s and 1960s. It is rather amazing that an elderly gentleman, Walter, walked the same route at the same time, day after day, year after year, with a bag of money and no one ever accosted him or mugged him. There was no need for a Brink's truck or armed guards. Des Plaines was his town, he knew many of the people there, and no one bore him any ill will. Walter was that kind of man, and Des Plaines was that kind of town.

Roger, Walter, Dave (left to right)

Ultimately, Roger returned to work to manage the men's department after getting a degree in Marketing at the University of Illinois in 1949 and David graduated from Arizona State University with a degree in Marketing and became co-manager of the men's department and was in charge of store advertising in 1951. Bob finished stints in the Navy and the Army and managed the women's department with his mother, Pearl. Gerry Weaver, who had married Louis Jr.'s youngest daughter Barbara in 1960, came to manage the household items department, fabric section, and women's accessories on the first floor. They were all competent and committed in their responsibilities and had the same cordial, friendly relations with employees which was Walter's style. Everyone got along very well at the store and staff enjoyed working there. As one employee put it, "I should pay Spiegler's because I enjoy working here so much."

Business meetings were generally held near the end of the work day in the basement when the men gathered around the luncheon table with a Scotch or Manhattan in hand. Employees may still be coming down to the basement stockroom to get merchandise for a last minute sale, the stock boy would be sweeping the floor, people leaving work would go to the refrigerator in the corner to grab their leftovers, and a child or two could be milling about waiting to be taken home. It was a very informal affair, so informal that, if you did not know them, well, you would not think it was a business meeting at all.

* * *

Grandpa (Walter) was quite a card player and his love of playing cards influenced the careers of two of his grandsons, Jake and Rick, to become professional gamblers. Grandpa Walter had a spacious basement with cement walls and a vinyl tile floor, and in this basement was a hexagonal poker table with green felt and six chairs. In fact, this was the only furniture I remember in his basement. Frequently he would have friends come over in the evening to play poker and pinochle.

When we were small boys we would go down the long wooden stairs into the basement and go exploring. We found there was a bathroom downstairs and there are two things I remember about the bathroom. One thing was that it always had a slight odor of sewage as the house and plumbing were so old that the sewer pipe had become somewhat blocked. The other thing we discovered was that the roll of toilet paper had jokes and cartoons on it. Grandpa had bought this so that when his friends needed to use the facilities they would have something to entertain themselves. Glenn and I would carefully unroll the toilet paper about four or five feet without tearing it and then we would look at all the cartoons and jokes. We got a big kick out of this. Then we would carefully roll the toilet paper back up (as careful as little boys can be) so that no one would know we had been there.

During the Prohibition Era from 1920 to 1932, the manufacture, distribution and sale of alcohol was forbidden. Many Americans never accepted Prohibition, however, and a large business of illegally making and selling alcohol grew by men called "bootleggers." Grandpa used to play cards with bootleggers. When Dad (Roger) was a boy, he observed this, and one day he asked his father, "Why do you play cards with gangsters?"

Grandpa replied, "They are businessmen just like I am. They just have a different kind of business."

* * *

Dorothy Mills, long-time office manager at the store, wrote a letter back to the store after she retired, reminiscing about the good times she had there. In the letter she recounts a joke she played on Walter one time, and I will summarize the first part of the story and then let Dorothy tell the climax in her own words.

Dorothy, her husband, her sister, and her sister's husband had gone on a vacation to Texas and stopped at a Stuckey's Restaurant on the expressway. While there she saw a postcard which made her laugh. There was a picture of "an old toothless, so called, hillbilly woman" with the quotation, "If no one claims me in thirty days, I'm yours." Seeing the funny card inspired Dorothy to conceive of a joke to play on Walter, who "was the oldest [of the Spiegler men] and one of the sweetest guys I know." Dorothy bought several of those postcards and mailed them to Walter starting in Texas and several other places on her way home. Walter received them at the store and was mystified who would be sending him this postcard from all these places, but he suspected that a salesman he knew was doing the prank. Walter asked the salesman if he was responsible for this, but the salesman denied any knowledge of the card. Walter could not figure it out. By this time, Dorothy had arrived back in Des Plaines and had come back to work. Dorothy tells what happened next in her letter.

"It was getting time for Halloween. Working at Spiegler's could be quite an experience at times, especially when fun and games were played at times. And this story is about one of those times.

When the last note was sent, I had written, 'See you soon.' The fellows always used to go to the corner restaurant for coffee so that day I went into the store all dressed up in a half mask, bathrobe, fur coat, and shopping bag with old scarf around my head and dark glasses, I sent one of the clerks over to tell Wally I was there. All his buddies came back with him and when I said in a funny voice, 'Mr. Spiegler,' he pointed to one of the other guys, but they all pointed back to him. I just couldn't help but laugh, and the cat was out of the bag. Well, no one thought Dorothy would ever do a thing like this. But they did not know me, did they? When I look at some of these pictures from the store I get a little lonesome for some of those good times we had there. So many wonderful memories to think about on a cold winter night as age creeps up on me. Thanks guys, all five of you that I worked with, you are some of the best."

Walter was a member of several civic and fraternal organizations. He was a life-long member of the Des Plaines Elks Club, a Mason and Shriner, and a member of the American Legion. He and Mabel would walk down Laurel Avenue on nice days to attend services at the First Congregational Church on Sunday. He also served on the Board of Directors of the First Federal Savings and Loan of Des Plaines for several decades.

Walter never was elected to any political office or served as leader of any organization. He did not seek roles of leadership like his older brother Victor. Yet, over time, he was recognized by many as an unofficial "elder" of the town of

Des Plaines. When he turned 79, he was interviewed by the *Suburban Times* in a substantial article on the move of the store to the new Des Plaines Mall and his perspectives on life in Des Plaines. In 1982 when Walter and Mabel celebrated their sixtieth wedding anniversary, there was a long article where they reminisced about their marriage and experiences as young people, Walter in town, and Mabel on the Busse farm.

When Walter was in his eighties, the *Suburban Times* also ran an article on whether senior citizens felt safe walking the streets, and Walter was one of the people interviewed. He was well-known in the community and people were interested in his opinion on things.

* * *

Walter at the wheel ca 1920

Grandpa (Walter) always drove Cadillacs. It was the one sign of wealth and ostentation he allowed himself. He owned stock in General Motors and he was a Cadillac man. And in the 1960's, the Cadillac was a big, long car with the biggest fins I have ever seen. It looked like it was ready to take off into Outer Space. Grandpa had a narrow cement driveway which skirted his brick house and led to a two-car garage. If Grandpa drove the car to the garage, he knew he would have to back that behemoth as straight as an arrow down the driveway to avoid scraping the side of the car against the house. He wisely decided just to park the car on the short strip of the driveway in front of the house to avoid that catastrophe. Besides, his brick garage which was built in 1924 was meant to accommodate a car like a Model A Ford, not the big car he was now driving.

Victor, his brother, and Pearl lived right next to Walter and Mabel in another brick house. Pearl's maiden name was Nagel, and her father had been part owner of the Kuhlman-Nagel Chrysler-Plymouth dealership, which used to be on Pearson Street. Pearl only drove Chrysler cars, and a Dodge or a Plymouth would not do. She had to drive the Chrysler Imperial, which was Chrysler's top of the line car and rivaled the Cadillac and Ford's Lincoln.

Now the 1960's could well be dubbed the Age of Chrome in American auto manufacturing. The luxury cars all had big chrome bumpers, big chrome grills, and the trim, door handles, mirrors, and doo-dads were all chrome. Chrome was the paramount symbol of American affluence. And Chrysler, to show it was at the top of the pack, had put so much chrome on the Imperial that it looked almost gaudy. In truth, the Imperial looked like a large bass lure coming down the road.

So, when you drove down Prairie Avenue, you saw Grandpa's big Cadillac sitting on his driveway in front of his house, and then you saw Pearl's big Imperial sitting on the driveway in front of her house. It always seemed to me that there was a rivalry going on, but no one ever talked about it.

In the 1970's the Chrysler Corporation experienced significant financial woes and it was only the business acumen of new CEO Lee Iacocca and a large loan from the U.S. government which saved the company. Mr. Iacocca scrapped the Imperial and started producing smaller, simpler, more fuel-efficient vehicles. The American public had weighed in on the issue, and they had sided with Grandpa and his Cadillac against Pearl. I guess after that Pearl had to drive New Yorkers.

* * *

Louis Jr.

Louis Jr. was born in 1910, the third son of Louis and Minnie Spiegler. Louis Sr. was to die of a stroke in 1918. Louis Jr. recalls that after this Walter acted as a second father to him. He fondly remembers that when he was a teenager Walter used to let him drive the delivery truck from the garage to the loading dock. The two brothers were to work together and go hunting and fishing together for all of their lives.

Walter and Louis on Canadian fishing trip. ca 1964

Even though Louis Jr. was a young boy, he worked in the store stocking shelves and making deliveries. All the members of the family worked at the store, and this included him.

The store was one of the few outlets in the northwest suburbs of Chicago where uniforms and equipment for the Cub Scout and Boy Scout programs could be purchased. Howard Richardson, who worked in the men's department for decades and was an avid supporter of the Scouts, was in charge of this section. The store began carrying scouting equipment in 1922 when Louis became a Boy Scout. From that time on, the store was always a major retail outlet for scouting equipment in the region.

Louis Jr. attended Knox College in Galesburg, Illinois after graduating from high school. He played on both of the football and basketball teams, and one year narrowly missed being named athlete of the year at the college.

When Louis attended college, he was given an old REO automobile by his brother. The car had originally belonged to his mother, Minnie. Roger recalls the REO was named after Robert E. Olds, who later created the Oldsmobile. Roger states that it was an ornate car which had slender flower vases fastened to the interior walls of the car where the owner could put cut flowers. It was a style, like rumble seats and hidden headlights, which never caught on with the American public.

A young Louis golfing, his passion. ca 1932

All three brothers enjoyed hunting and fishing, but Louis was the most athletic. Once he returned to Des Plaines from college, he took up golf as his major sport and was a long-time member of Park Ridge Country Club. Shirley recalls that he was also an excellent dancer.

Louis Jr. was tall, trim and handsome. His looks took after those of his father. He married Harriet Thompson in 1932 and they had two daughters, Carol and Barbara.

Carol states that her father was always there for his family. Although Harriet was the person who they went to in order to solve everyday problems and concerns, their father was their foundation, "the rock" of the family.

Carol states that a photograph taken of the family while on the beach at Lake Michigan as young girls portrays the family constellation well. Carol was serenely leaning against her father's side, but her parents were neither looking at her or at the water. Their heads and eyes were turned in the opposite direction, looking at Barbara who had run off and was about to get into trouble. Barbara was the active, adventurous one, and her parents had learned early on to always keep their eyes on her.

When Louis returned from Knox College, he became the manager of the grocery department. Carol recalls that he was color-blind and was not suited to sell men's clothing for this reason. When the grocery department was closed in 1947, he worked in the basement in shipping and receiving with Walter. Walter and Louis worked together for over sixty years.

Louis filled the void of community leadership left by the death of Victor and was very active in the business community and in civic organizations. He was a life-long member of the Lions Club and served as president. He also was president of the Chamber of Commerce one year. He was on the Board of Directors of the First National Bank of Des Plaines for several decades and supported local businesses in this capacity.

*Louis representing the First National Bank
with Walter Morava at inception of the
Morava Stationery Store, 1960*

Louis' first wife Harriet, died of cancer in 1975. In 1978 he married Edith Bender, a widow. When Edith was a younger woman, she was an Olympic-quality fencing instructor. In this marriage Louis inherited many step-children and step-grandchildren whom he thoroughly enjoyed in his later years.

In 2007 Roger, Jay, and his wife Fran visited Louis in his home. As we chatted around the kitchen table, Louis lighted up a cigarette and said somewhat defensively, "I have been smoking since I was fifteen and I'm not going to stop now." How do you argue about the health benefits of stopping smoking with a man who is 97? We continued to chat for a while and as it approached noontime, Louis announced that he always has a Manhattan at noon and he got up to go prepare one. We felt this was our cue to leave.

When we got home, I remarked to my mother that we had a nice visit with Louis and we left when he was going to have a Manhattan. My mother replied, "Oh. That is a switch. He always used to have two Manhattans at noon."

CHAPTER 5

THE GREAT DEPRESSION AND WORLD WAR II

WW1 veterans prepare to join "Bonus Army" to march on Washington D.C. to demand promised bonus. An unsympathetic President Hoover sent Col. Douglas MacArthur and Army to disperse the marchers. ca1930

  The Great Depression began on Black Thursday in October of 1929. The prosperity and good times of the Roaring Twenties were over. The economies of European nations were already depressed due to the destruction and huge debts created by the First World War and the effects of this began spilling over to the United States. European nations had erected high tariff walls to the products of American agriculture and some manufacturing, and the American farm economy had been depressed for some time. Now the nation as a whole was to experience a severe economic depression.

The sell-off of equities in the stock market on Black Thursday sparked a sense of panic among ordinary citizens and business leaders alike. People stormed the banks to withdraw their money before the banks ran out of funds and closed their doors. Hundreds of banks went out of business and many people lost their life savings.

As people hunkered down out of anxiety and stopped spending money, businesses stopped selling products and began laying off employees. The economic situation spiraled downward and the conservative fiscal policies of President Hoover were unable to restore people's confidence. By 1932, over twelve-million laborers were unemployed, about 25% of the workforce. There was not only economic depression, but a depression of the morale of the American people as a whole. Although the New Deal programs of the new President Roosevelt were able to restore some of this morale, full employment was not to return to the nation until World War II.

The store managed to keep its doors open while many other businesses failed, but there was a reduction in staff. The family members continued to manage their respective departments, but Bob states that in order to deal with the reduction in staff, the store initiated a new concept of self-service where customers browsed in the store and selected the merchandise they wanted and then were rung out. This sales method is used by many modern businesses today.

Roger recalls that the store during this era had a flour room which stored fifty-pound bags of flour for people to buy. There was a delivery truck which delivered the bag of flour to people's homes. Bread was a staple food at that time and many people baked their own bread as it was economical and nutritious. This was a way people could save some money.

Shirley spoke about growing up during the Depression of the 1930's. She said that sometimes the township had no money to pay the school teachers, and for their salary they received written IOU's or promissory notes called 'scrip'. The teachers would bring this scrip to the store to purchase clothing and food. At a later date when the township had money the store would redeem the scrip for cash. The town made it through the Depression because the school board, the teachers, and the merchants all worked together so this system would function. Do you think if a teacher went into Macy's or J.C. Penney today with a written IOU that the management would allow them to purchase merchandise with it? Highly unlikely.

Remodeled Spiegler Store next to City Hall, ca 1936.

Johnson, in his book on the history of Des Plaines, states, "During the 1930's Spiegler's acted as an anchor to windward in a business district that was severely depressed due to the uncertain state of the nation's economy. Indeed, the Spiegler family's confidence in the city's future remained undiminished."[1]

---

1. Johnson, Donald S. Des Plaines: Born of the Tall Grass Prairie. (Windsor Publications: Woodhaven, California, 1984) p. 50

Many people were out of work and when they came to the store to purchase food, clothing, and other necessities, they did not have the money to pay. Victor, knowing the circumstances of the family, would say, "It's on your tab," and then never seek to collect the debt. There was little in terms of government relief during this era and people had to stick together to help each other.

Minnie was optimistic for the prospects of the store, the town, and the nation and in 1935 she instituted a complete renovation of the store, inside and out. An interior passage way was made between the men's department, which was in a separate building, and the main store. New counters and displays were put in. The new facade of the store was done in art-deco style, which was the predominant architectural style of the time.

Des Plaines shared this optimism, and two years later the town tore down the old village hall and fire department which stood on the corner of Lee and Ellinwood Streets near the store and erected the structure across the railroad tracks on Miner Street.

On December 7, 1941 the Japanese fleet attacked Pearl Harbor in Hawaii with warplanes launched off aircraft carriers and the United States entered World War II, which already had been raging in Europe for two years. President Roosevelt, in his radio address to the nation, declared the attack "a day which will go down in infamy," and committed the full strength of the country to defeat Japan. Germany and Italy, allies of Japan, quickly declared war on the United States. Over eleven-million American men and women served in the armed forces during the conflict and millions more were employed in factories and farms to equip and feed the armed forces. Full employment returned to the country and the morale of the country was committed to defeating the Axis powers. Full employment meant that people could afford housing, food and clothing, but the standard of living was not high for most laborers and farmers as the government was paying for the war effort by going into debt by selling war bonds.

Bob states that during the Great Depression the problem for retail stores was that customers had little money due to unemployment or low wages, but during World War II the problem for retailers was finding enough products to sell. Many industries had diverted their time and energy from producing consumer goods to producing material needed for the war effort, be it food, stockings, or tanks. Metals such as iron, copper, tungsten and aluminum were all in short supply as they were needed to build ships, war planes, and many other items used in the war. Even staple food items such as meat, sugar and coffee were rationed and the customer had to present coupons to get their allotment.

The managers, Minnie, Victor, Walter and Louis had to search high and low among manufacturers to find a sufficient variety of items to stock the shelves. People on the whole accepted the fact that there was not a great variety of items to buy at the store. Although many large industries making war material made large profits during the war, smaller retailers had difficulty staying in business.

Minnie Spiegler died in early 1944 after working a full day at the store and retiring to her apartment. She led a simple life materially that was devoted to the business, her family, and the community. She never had a house built for herself, but lived her whole life in an apartment. She never spent her money on luxury, but always put it back into the business or gave it to her sons to help Victor and Walter build their homes and send Louis to college.

After forty-four years serving the community she was well-liked and respected, and a long retinue of cars accompanied her casket to the Town of Maine cemetery where she was buried next to the grave of her husband, Louis.

The Depression and World War II

Minnie's death left the business and the family in a crisis. She was the manager and buyer of the women's department, the largest department of the store. Women always do most of the buying in the apparel business. Bob states that without a buyer for the women's department, the family began to consider other options and had contacted Butler Brothers to consider becoming a Ben Franklin 5¢ and 10¢ store. It was possible they might close the store.

Gravesite of Louis Sr. and Minnie

During this crisis, it was Pearl, Victor's wife, who stepped up to the plate. She was an intelligent, personable and competent woman who had come from a business family. She was very familiar with the operation of the store from Victor, and had an eye for women's clothing and accessories. She became the manager and chief buyer for the women's department and even after Victor's death in 1954, she continued on in this capacity and was an officer in the company for several decades.

It would be easy to see the story of the store and the family as a story about men. The general store was begun by two brothers, Louis and Benjamin, inherited by Louis' three sons, and then the third generation consisted of three sons who worked there as managers and were heads of the company. But focusing on the male leadership in the family would not give the complete picture. It was the women of the family, Minnie and Pearl, who stepped forward at the times of crisis to insure the continuance of the store and avoid its closing: Minnie upon the death of her husband Louis in 1918 and Pearl when Minnie died in 1944. Without these capable, bright women, the store would have closed and the family splintered without this economic and social point of focus.

Pearl functioned as the matriarch of the family business for many years and had an interesting history and unique personality. Born in 1902 in a farmhouse on the Des Plaines River, her mother died when she was very young and her mother's sister, Ella, came to live in the home to care for Pearl. To avoid scandal, Pearl's father, Fred Nagel, married Ella and they remained married until his death.

Unlike some of the Spieglers, Pearl was a cosmopolitan spirit and her love of life and adventure could not be contained within the boundaries of Des Plaines. After her husband's death, she joined a travel group and became a world traveler when not minding the store. She rode on a camel past the Egyptian pyramids, floated down the Nile on a barge, and traveled to the cold climate of Point Barrow, Alaska. When in Ireland, she bent over backwards to kiss the blarney stone and nearly couldn't get up. She ventured to Tahiti and stayed in a hut, but found the heat and humidity so oppressive she tore off the sleeves of all her blouses so she could be cooler.

Pearl's grandchildren and great-grandchildren referred to her as "Grandma Peachy" as she was so generous to them. When she returned from a trip, she would have something special for them from the country she had traveled to, such as dolls, jewelry, and traditional clothes.

CHAPTER 6

MABEL AND THE BUSSE CONNECTION

When Mabel Busse moved off of the farm to marry Walter Spiegler in 1922 and came to the town of Des Plaines, an important connection was formed between the two families. Roger has warm memories of motoring into Chicago to visit with the Spiegler and Baer families on some weekends, and then on other weekends going to the Busse farm on the corner of Busse Road and Algonquin Road in Mt. Prospect to visit with his mother's family. Mabel had lived with her parents, Martin and Doris Busse and her six siblings on the original farmstead of Henry Busse, the German pioneer who first came to America in 1847 seeking a better life. Shirley remembers some of the unique people she knew then, such as her great-grandmother who wore a black stovepipe hat. As children, we attended the reunions and picnics of the Busse family held at Busse Woods which were always a part of the Spiegler family tradition.

The story of the settling of the Busse family in northwest Cook County is interesting in its own right, and is well described in the book *The Busse Family in America 1848 – 1998.* The Busse family were mainly farmers in their early days in America. One thing which is noteworthy about the family is the large number of descendants of Henry's parents, Frederick and Johanna, which currently number over 5,000. Over 2,500 family members attended the family reunion held at the Lake County Fairgrounds in 1998, and the event is recorded in the *Guinness Book of Records.*

The Busse family also played an important part in the creation of the town of Mount Prospect and were a prominent business family. None of this would have happened without the pioneering efforts of Henry Busse.

Homestead of Henry and son Martin Busse (left to right) Mabel Busse Spiegler in baby carriage, mother Doris standing, Henry and Mary seated with grand-daughter Gertrude in between, Martin and son Elmer in carriage, 1900.

Henry Busse was born in 1828, the third child of Frederick and Johanna. The family, which included six children in all, lived in a small village outside of Hanover, Germany, and Frederick owned a little farm. Life was difficult for the Busses economically, as it was for many Germans, and a social revolution was to erupt in 1848. Discontent was high and many sought to find a better life in North and South America.

Henry has been characterized by some family members as "part pioneer, part rogue, and part nomad." As there was not much good farmland available in the country, it was the custom that the eldest son would inherit the property and the younger brothers would have to settle with being tradesmen or farm laborers. Henry's older brother Christian, was destined to inherit the farm. Henry, who was a person of big dreams and a penchant to see foreign lands, was not satisfied with these prospects for himself. He had heard that America had abundant land for farming and offered the opportunity for a prosperous life. At age nineteen, he spoke with his father about his desire to travel to America to see if this was indeed true, and promised he would write about the results of his findings.

Henry journeyed with his long-time friend, Christian Henjes, by ship to the United States and then by train and wagon to the Midwest. They found work as farmhands on a farm in Sheboygan, Wisconsin and Henry began writing letters back to his family. He was favorably impressed by what he found in the country. There was wide open country and abundant farmland which could be bought inexpensively. People in America came from a variety of European countries and the social climate was accepting. Henry also found that the climate was one of peace, unlike a turbulent Europe where kings and nobles were frequently warring with each other and young men were involuntarily conscripted into the army. He felt this would be a good place for the family to settle and begin a new life.

Back in Germany, the Busse family read Henry's letters with enthusiasm and were encouraged by his reports about this new land. There was little opportunity for advancement in Germany at this time due to a lack of available land and a rigid class structure and little room for optimism and hope of a better life. After much reflection and discussion, the family decided that the time to move was now. The farm and most of their possessions were sold and the voyage to

America was made with some of their clothing, personal items and tools.

The family met Henry in Chicago in early 1848 and began a trek by foot carrying some of their possessions in a wheelbarrow, looking for good farmland. After walking to Hanover Township and not finding the clay soil to their liking, they finally purchased a farm from an innkeeper where they stayed one night on an old Indian trail which was to become Algonquin Road in Mt. Prospect at a later date.

Henry was glad to see his family and happy they had decided to join him in settling in America, but he had no farm himself or money to purchase one. It would take a long time, if ever, to earn enough money as a farmhand to purchase a farm. It was at this time that Henry began to hear reports of gold, precious gold, being discovered in a distant place called California on the Pacific coast. This land had only been ceded to the United States three years previously as a result of the Mexican-American War. Henry became convinced that going to California and becoming a forty-niner would be his best chance to earn the money he needed to purchase a farm.

Henry spoke about his plans with his friend Christian and another young man, and all three decided to go westward to look for gold and quick fortune. They set out in a wagon train in April of 1848 for California, a trip which would take over six months. The only things Henry carried with him were a knapsack, a lantern, and a gun to defend himself from hostile Native Americans and claims jumpers in California. The wagon train forded streams, climbed mountains, crossed arid desert and some members of the party died during the trip, but in October the three companions finally arrived in California.

Henry and his friends did strike a claim and panned for gold, looking for golden nuggets among the pebbles in their sluices and pans. Although they did not make a fortune, they made a sufficient amount of money to satisfy their needs. Henry and Christian decided not to make the long tedious journey overland through hostile Indian territory again, but instead took a sailing ship to the Isthmus of Panama, hiked over the Andes Mountains, and then took another ship to New Orleans. A riverboat took them northward up the Mississippi River back to Illinois and home. Just imagine doing all of that by the time you were twenty-one.

Henry arrived back at his parents' farm with about $6,000 in gold which was enough money to purchase a parcel of land just to the south of their farm. Within a few years he was to wed a pretty adolescent girl named Mary Behrens and begin a family. Henry had been cured of his wanderlust and settled down to farm the land and raise seven children.

As Henry grew older, his youngest son Martin took over management of the farm and Martin, with his wife Doris, raised eight children on the homestead, including Mabel. His granddaughter Mabel recalled many of Henry's stories of adventure and sayings because Henry lived to a ripe old age of eighty-nine and died in 1917, the same year when Mabel met Walter Spiegler at a Halloween dance. One thing she remembered her grandfather say several times was that whenever there was a skirmish between the new settlers and the Native Americans, it was always the settlers which began the conflict. Her grandfather also told her that sometimes when he was asleep on the trail to California the rats would nibble on his toes.

Martin and Doris Busse, ca 1894.

Martin Busse farm truck.

Mabel had fond memories of her family and the farm while growing up, but she said that it was a lot of work and they bore considerable personal discomfort. Like many children raised on a farm in those days, Mabel only attended school until the eighth grade, but it was not like she was allowed to lay around after she turned thirteen. She and her sisters helped their mother each day prepare meals for the farmhands. After they had prepared lunch, they carried it to the laborers in the fields. They then returned to the house to prepare supper for everyone, the main meal of the day. Bread dough had to be kneaded and then baked in an iron cook stove heated with wood finely chopped. Piles of potatoes were peeled and chickens were plucked of feathers to be eaten. All the farm animals needed to be tended and fed on a daily basis. In the warmer months the girls worked in the gardens and helped their mother can fruit and vegetables for the winter. Wash for nine people was all done by hand with a washtub, washboard and soap, and the washed clothes were hung on long lines to dry. And then there were those long walks in the winter through cold and snow to sit on a frozen plank in the outhouse to do one's business as quickly as possible and hurry back to a warm house. In an interview with the *Suburban Times* commemorating their sixtieth wedding anniversary, Mabel said that "the good old days" were highly romanticized and she preferred the comforts and conveniences of modern society.

Roger remembers the visits to his mother's family on the farm. When they ate dinner, his grandfather Martin would always eat a full plate of potatoes before anything else. He would cut the potatoes up with a fork and eat them all before eating a new plate with meat, vegetables, and bread. Roger said he knew when his grandfather was getting older and weaker when he would not eat as many potatoes with his meal.

Shirley on the farm, 1926.

Shirley wrote about her mother Mabel's family in her paper entitled "My People." She wrote:

"The Great Grandma Willie I knew might have been teleported from the late 1800's. I never questioned her dress during the twenty years that I knew her; but, now that it is too late, my curiosity is aroused. I assume that the black stovepipe hat perched on her gray bun had been hers for decades. She made her own ankle-length, full-skirted dresses and coats (usually black), but why didn't her daughters try to change her mode of dress? Did they try, or did they just accept? And where did she buy those high, black, laced shoes?

"My Grandpa Busse, a German Lutheran, living in a German Lutheran community, sent his seven children to "English" school for the first four years, was forced (probably by my grandmother) to send them to German Lutheran school for the next four so that they might be confirmed, and then made them repeat eighth grade in the public school. He insisted that the parochial school spent so much time in teaching religion and German that the children didn't receive an education. In that farming community, this was heresy."

* * *

Jay recalls, "Upstairs on the second floor of my grandparents' (Walter and Mabel) home was a small walk-in closet which I found one day while exploring as a young boy. It was an odd-shaped little room under one corner of the roof. In it I found a variety of items such as an old lamp, some boxes of books, clothing and flower pots. As I was looking at those items I came across an old newspaper which was tan with age. The headlines of the *Chicago Tribune* read something like "V-E Day! Germany Unconditionally Surrenders" and it was dated May 8, 1945. On the front page was a small picture of General Dwight D. Eisenhower in his military uniform and another picture of Adolf Hitler. I was becoming a fan of history at the time and found the newspaper interesting, so I took it downstairs and asked Grandma if I could take it home to look at it. She agreed, and after I looked at it for a week, Dad returned it to her.

As a young boy I wondered why she had kept a newspaper that was so old. It was the only old newspaper she had. Certainly it was an important date to remember, but there were many important historical events which had occurred in her lifetime. Why did she keep this newspaper? It was only as I grew older and was a man that I understood why the newspaper was important to her. Her son had been fighting in Europe for nine months and she was terribly worried he would be injured or killed. Many men had lost their lives in the war, including men from Des Plaines and the area. The local newspaper carried the news of their deaths. Every day Grandma prayed that her son would return home safely from the war, and every day she dreaded that a uniformed man would pull into her driveway in a black car and inform her that her son had been killed. The day she received that newspaper was probably one of the happiest days of her life."

* * *

Walter and Mabel had an open front porch to their house and the porch and cement steps descending to the sidewalk were covered with a bright green indoor-outdoor carpet. They would sit on the front porch during nice weather and greet people when they walked by.

One day Dad (Roger) came home and was upset with his mother. He had visited her after work and found her on her knees mending some tears in the carpet on the porch stairs with a needle and thread. He said he had told his mother they had enough money to replace the carpet, but she insisted that it was in relatively good shape and she could repair it. He left his mother still on her knees mending the carpet.

Grandma had grown up on a farm where they did not have much in terms of material possessions and what they possessed was only attained through hard work. They had learned to be self-sufficient and anything of value which was broken was either repaired or put to another use. To throw things away which could be repaired was considered wasteful, if not sinful. Grandma had learned the values of thrift and material simplicity on the farm and continued to live these values all of her life.

***

The summer of each year Mabel and Walter traveled to Florida to visit Mabel's youngest sister, Olive, who had married a man named Emil Schweppe and retired to Florida. Mabel had never learned how to drive an automobile and refused to travel by ship or airplane because ships like the Titanic can sink and airplanes can crash. But once a year she felt comfortable leaving Des Plaines to see a different part of the country with Walter driving his big Cadillac.

I would not have remembered their annual pilgrimage to Florida except for what they brought back for their grandchildren. They would purchase all sorts of unique items not found in Illinois like bright Bahamian sport shirts, large straw hats, maracas, rubber shrunken heads, stuffed baby alligators and alligator belts, Chinese handcuffs and miniature brass cannons. And then coming back from Florida they would stop in Tennessee where the sale of fireworks was legal, and purchase all kinds of bottle rockets, sparklers, snakes, firecrackers and cherry bombs, perhaps to the chagrin of our parents. Yes, a young child would remember their trips to Florida.

And it was in the giving of these gifts that we knew our grandparents cared.

They were not verbally or physically demonstrative people who gave lots of hugs and kisses. This was not part of their cultural upbringing or personalities. But in these gifts we knew they were always thinking of us and loved us.

* * *

This letter was sent by Jake to his cousins after the death of their grandmother Mabel in December of 1991.

"A new year, a new cousins' letter. This new year is the first year to open without Grandma May. She was, nearly, the last Spiegler of her generation (since Louis, born on the cusp, is as much a part of our parents' generation as he is a part of her generation). She was our last indirect link with our German heritage; our last direct link with the 19th Century. She was six months old when the 20th Century began, three years old when the Wright Brothers flew, and *The Great Train Robbery* was creating a stir in what passed for movie theaters. By the time she reached my age, she had lived through World War I, the Twenties, and most of the Depression; two of her children were in high school, and all this was still three years before Pearl Harbor. Beyond all of this, she was our last common ancestor.

"All the Spieglers of Grandma's generation made a career of working at Spiegler's, and all of them lived in Des Plaines. Most of our parent's generation did the same; and with the exception of Gerry and Barbara Weaver, stayed in the State of Illinois. Now, the store is no longer owned by the family, and only three of the ten cousins live in the Chicago area. By the beginning of the Twenty-first Century there may be no Spieglers still living in Illinois, and no public display of the name in Des Plaines except for an obscure and faded metal plaque mounted on a rock near the river bank.

"It is common now to define people in terms of their careers (though a disproportionate number of us cousins make such definition difficult. Perhaps we are part of the "ineffable generation", eh, Tracy?) But Grandma May, in common with her generation, had no career. The configuration of her life is instead defined by her singular product: her children and grandchildren. If we are to continue as a family, reuniting even in unexpected places (sorry I missed you in Hong Kong, Jenny), sharing bits of common memory and outlook, it is because she did her life's work well. Whenever any two of us are together, some part of her will continue to live. In that sense perhaps we can accomplish for her what her own tired flesh could not: carry some vital part of her spirit onward into a third century."

—Jake

CHAPTER 7

The Third Generation and Post-War Era

After World War II, the United States experienced a time of prosperity. Much of the industrial base of Europe and Japan had been destroyed, and the United States emerged as the dominant political and economic power of the world. This prosperity was shared by the people of Des Plaines and the success of the store. Victor, Walter, and Louis Jr. all had children who had worked at some time in their lives in the store, particularly the men. To be a Spiegler meant to work at the store and it was the economic and psychological center of the whole family.

Spiegler family, 1955. Victor, Pearl's husband, had died in 1954. (left to right) Gail and Dave, Elaine and Roger, Mary and Bob, Pearl, Harriet and Louis, Mabel and Walter

Like the first and second generations, the children of Victor, Walter and Louis Jr. remained very involved in business and civic organizations and church. In running the store to supply people's needs and their involvement in these organizations, they contributed significantly to the community of Des Plaines and surrounding areas.

Shirley

Shirley, the daughter of Walter and Mabel, was the oldest child of the third generation. Bright and creative, she graduated from Maine East High School near the top of her class in 1940. She continued living at home and worked as a bookkeeper in the business office of the store from this time until her marriage in 1952. Even in her nineties, Shirley recalled with pleasure interacting with friends who would come to visit her in the office.

Shirley always had an interest in literature and theatre, and met her husband Bill Jacobs while doing dramatic performances in the Des Plaines Theatre Guild. A long-time friend of Bill's, Robert Donley, who also had an interest in acting, had introduced the couple while acting in the Guild. Bill and Bob had acted together in dramatic performances since the seventh grade, and were law partners in Des Plaines from 1953 – 1966.

Bill's family had moved to Des Plaines in 1938. He served as a lieutenant in the army after the war for two years and then graduated from Northwestern University with a bachelor's degree in speech and his law degree.

THE THIRD GENERATION

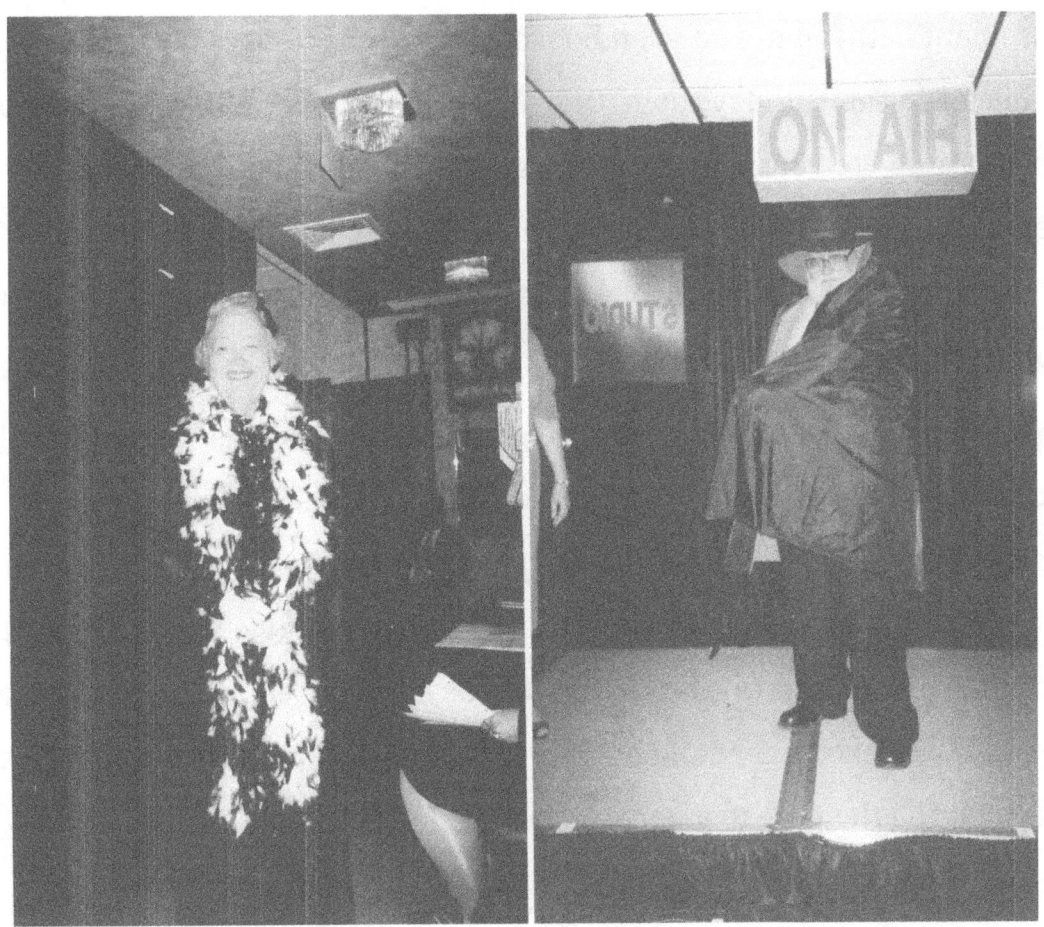

Shirley and Bill in theatre.

He served as alderman in Des Plaines in the 1950's and was the youngest person to be elected to this position. In 1964 he ran for the office of Judge of the Circuit Court in Cook County on the Republican slate, but Mayor Daley and his machine had ways of insuring that Democratic candidates won elections and Bill lost a hard-fought contest.

Shirley and Bill bought the house across the street from Walter and Mabel on the corner of Prairie and Laurel Avenue, and had three sons, Jake, Rick and Bruce. To enter this home was to enter a world of books and literature. There were law books lining the walls of Bill's study, books next to the fireplace in the living room, books on shelves in the basement, books stacked high on the commode in the basement bathroom, and even books in cardboard boxes laying near the hot water heater in the laundry room. One of Bill's interests was traveling across the country to pulp conventions and buying even more books. Jake could normally be seen strolling around the house with a paperback book in hand, and Bill was quick to respond on the latest book he read on human relationships and sexuality, part of his trade as a divorce lawyer.

One special memory I have was a gathering at the house as young children over the Christmas season to listen to a dramatic presentation of the novel *The Portrait of Dorian Gray* by Bill. Bill, being a speech major and actor with a deep, resonant voice, knew how to be dramatic. We met several times as Bill portrayed the horrible changes in Dorian Gray's soul as symbolized by the portrait of him in the attic with excitement and horror. Looking back on those days, I can appreciate Bill taking the time to entertain us and share with us his love of literature.

Shirley played the role of dutiful wife and mother well and worked as legal secretary for Bill, but her bright spirit was not content with this. As her sons became adults, she decided to go to Oakton Community College to earn a degree in theatre and become a professional actress. It takes a special person to do this in her fifties, and Shirley felt embarrassed at times by being in classes with students who were thirty years younger than her. Although she never burned her bra in the streets, she was as much the feminist as her grandmother Minnie, whom she admired. She worked as a professional actress for twenty-five years, working for advertising firms, government, and acting on some television programs such as *Early Edition*.

Shirley doing an ad for Sun Computers in Chicago.

Shirley and Bill hosted a public access television program reviewing Chicago theatre in the 1980's. She also co-produced and directed a dramatic presentation of the history of Des Plaines for the sesquicentennial celebration in 1985.

Roger

Roger was the second born son of Walter and Mabel. When he graduated from Maine East High School in 1942 he was immediately drafted into the army to fight in World War II. He was stationed at Ft. Bowie, Texas, in Wichita, and Ft. Graber, Oklahoma before embarking to Europe to fight the Germans in September of 1944. He was assigned to a heavy mortar company of the 42nd Rainbow Division, Seventh Army.

While in Kansas, Roger took some college courses and was offered a commission to become an officer. He had heard that the enemy always tried to kill the officers of a unit first, and he declined the commission. He felt it was better to be a live private than a dead hero.

While stationed in the United States, Roger exchanged frequent letters with his older sister, Shirley, which she kept after the war and gave back to him. In a letter from Ft. Gruber in July of 1944 Roger told the following joke which he had heard from other servicemen. It was interesting that Roger would tell an off-color joke to his older sister, but they were close, it was wartime, and the family always was down-to-earth. Here is the joke:

"Did you hear about the Ski Trooper who just got back from his first furlough in two years? He was a married guy and when he returned with his furlough papers, his commanding officer said, 'I won't ask you what the first thing was you did when you got home. What was the second thing you did?' The Ski Trooper promptly replied, 'I took off my skis.'"

The Seventh Army landed in Marseilles, France in September of 1944 and were warmly greeted by crowds of French citizens. They marched northward through Vichy, France and dug into positions in the Vosges Mountains in Alsace-Lorraine facing the German Siegfried Line. They held these positions against

German attacks as the Battle of the Bulge raged north of them in the Ardennes Forest of Belgium.

One of Roger's duties was to lug around a 45-pound piece of a heavy mortar and assemble the mortar to fire. He said most of the men and their replacements in his company were killed. It was only those who learned the necessary survival skills quickly who made it to the end of the war. There were times when the fighting was so intense that they could not shower for several weeks and occasionally a truck would come by with new underwear so they could change and discard the old ones.

The Division entered Germany through Strasbourg and captured Munich at the end of the war. Units of the Division liberated the infamous Dachau Concentration Camp, but Roger did not enter the camp. He said he saw the former prisoners dressed in rags wandering around the city looking somewhat bewildered. Hunger was widespread among former prisoners and German citizens at the end of the war. They would approach the American soldiers and ask for the K-rations that the soldiers were not going to finish. Roger always gave them his leftover food, but he said not all soldiers would do this.

Roger in Austria at end of European theatre, 1945.

Roger returned from Europe at the end of the war and began attending the University of Illinois on the G.I. Bill. He renewed a relationship with Elaine Partridge who he knew from high school and they were married in 1947. He graduated from the university in 1949 with a degree in marketing and came to manage the men's department, relieving his father. They had three sons named Jay, Glenn and Tracy, a part of the baby boom generation.

Roger was very active in civic organizations and gave a lot to the community of Des Plaines. He was a life-long Elk, as his father was, and served as Exalted Ruler of the Des Plaines Elks Club in 1960. This club was both a social and service organization which raised money to help the needy. Roger was also in the Lions Club and every year worked at the pancake breakfast fundraiser at Maine West High School making huge pancakes which we had difficulty finishing. He served as president of the Chamber of Commerce and was selected to serve on the Board of Directors of the Des Plaines National Bank in 1974.

Roger with Bob Bade being installed as new President of Des Plaines Chamber of Commerce, 1994.

Robert

Robert was born in 1928 and was the only child of Victor and Pearl. Although the Spiegler family tended to be a mellow and happy lot, he was among the happiest. He could often be seen strolling around the store with a smile on his face, whistling a tune or with a good word to someone. Although technically he was our father's first cousin, we always referred to him as "Uncle Bob" out of respect and affection.

As a teenager and young adult Bob was skilled in carpentry, plumbing and electrical work. He completely remodeled his parents' basement and built much of the wooden shelving units which held merchandise in the stockroom in the basement. He also constructed props for the display windows facing Ellinwood Street. When he was manager of the women's department, he was skilled in dressing the mannequins and creating displays. Townspeople often looked forward to the seasonal changes in displays exhibited in the windows.

When working as a paperboy, Bob befriended a wealthy woman who lived on an estate on the Des Plaines River. Bob told her once that he would like to have a house on the river one day and the lady told him she would sell him a parcel. Bob worked hard to earn the money to buy the land and was able to purchase a lot while in high school. As an adult he contracted with an architect who had worked under Frank Lloyd Wright to design a house on the lot and moved there with his family in 1955.

Bob served in the Army and the Navy after the war. When working at the store he met a beautiful young salesclerk named Mary Gardner who he came to know and marry. When married he enlisted in the army and the two moved to Virginia where he worked as a medic. Mary and Bob had two children, Nancy and Susan.

Bob returned to work at the store again after the death of his father and he co-managed the women's department with his mother. In any department store, the women's department is the biggest and most important, as women buy much more apparel and household items than men.

THE THIRD GENERATION

In 1960 the store underwent a major renovation. It was important to be able to compete with the larger department stores like Marshall Fields and Carson Pirie Scott. The women's department on the second floor of the store was completely modernized with new fixtures and lighting. A rather elegant staircase was built to the second floor and an elevator put in, which Bob states was the second elevator in Des Plaines. In the men's department the shoe section was replaced by a large area to sell suits and sport coats. The facade of the store was completely redone and the older art deco-style lettering was removed.

(left to right) Louis, Dave, Bob, Kurt, and models atop float in Des Plaines Sesquicentennial Parade, ca 1985.

Bob was a life-long member of the Lions Club and served as president of the organization. He also served as President of the Chamber of Commerce. He was active in the First Congregational Church and served as trustee for a number of years. Like his father, he served as a volunteer fireman for many years. He was an Elk, a Mason and a Shriner. He enjoyed golf, boating and swimming at the local YMCA.

Bob after retirement

David

David, the third child of Walter and Mabel, was born in 1929 at the start of the Great Depression. He was delivered on the kitchen table of their home, a practice not uncommon in that era. This was the time-honored tradition of mothers giving birth in most agricultural communities where hospitals and doctors were not readily available. The expectant mother was supported and coached by older women in the family, and perhaps by a midwife.

David said that when he was a young boy and hanging around the store, his father used to put a pole across his shoulders with a bucket at each end of the pole. David would walk across Lee Street to Romano's Tavern where the buckets were filled with beer and then he would return to the store so the family and employees could all enjoy a cold beer.

David and Bob used to pal around together being of similar age. Bob recalls that they often would go fishing at the No. 2 Dam on the Des Plaines River, sometimes meeting up with the sons of bootlegger Roger Touhy. The distinctions which people make today between law-abiding citizens and gangsters were often not observed at that time.

The Ziehn family lived in a first floor apartment under the apartment of Minnie Spiegler in the building facing Lee Street and they ran a delicatessen out of the front of the building. Mrs. Ziehn was good friends with Minnie and they took a trip to California together. Buddy and Grace were the children of Charles and Gertrude Ziehn and Buddy was a great friend of Louis Jr. Grace was to become David's mother-in-law.

Gail, Grace's daughter, used to visit her grandparents at their place behind the delicatessen. She recalls, "I faintly remember the grocery department. I also remember David delivering groceries to my grandmother. I thought he was cute. I was probably eleven and David sixteen." So we learn that love sends its sparks even over a head of cabbage. Little did David know that he was a marked man after that point in time.

David had severe asthma as a boy and his parents sent him to Arizona State University in Tempe because of the low humidity and few allergens in the area. He graduated with a degree in marketing in 1951 and returned to Des Plaines to co-manage the men's department with Roger and handle the advertising of the store.

Grace, who worked in the women's section for many years, recruited her daughter Gail to work in the baby department one Christmas. The baby department was right next to the men's department at that time and Gail had time when sales were slow to venture over and get to know David. We all know where this story is heading, and they were married in 1953.

Dave in Rockies after retirement.

David and Gail had four children: Karla, Kurt, Jenny, and Mary. After living in Des Plaines for a while, they moved to rural Wauconda and had a home built on a small lake. Despite his asthma, David was a great outdoors man and loved to boat, fish, hunt, garden, bicycle and cross-country ski. As children we spent a great deal of time at their home to see family and hunt and ice-skate in the winter, and swim and sail on the lake in the summer.

The Third Generation

Dave teaching great-nephews and great niece how to fish at Timberlake.

David continued being active in business and civic organizations despite the fact he lived some distance from the city. He was a board member of Holy Family Hospital and the Chamber of Commerce. After his father retired, David was selected to be on the Board of Directors of a reconfigured First Federal Savings and Loan. He also served as president of the Lions Club and was on the board.

If A Store Could Talk... The Spiegler Family Remembers

This poem was written by Jenny to commemorate the twenty-fifth wedding anniversary of her parents David and Gail. She states, "As one of their four children, I can only be thankful that they raised us in the manner they did. They gave us the opportunity to experience a lot of life's great moments, with guidance into some of the better corners. 'Excerpts From A Moment In Time' is an expression of my gratitude to them, and an interpretation of these moments."

Behind your eyes, there is an entire
universe of thought,
And I can only see the glimmer
of escaping rays.

Everything in the past has led to a certain
level of understanding and relating.
You've given me something that means a lot more
than anything I can touch or hold.
And even when we're not together
there will be a lasting bond of friendship,
strengthened by memories.
Just between us and a few years time.

I'm a lot wiser now and you might say I've changed.
Well you've changed too, but my memories of you
remain the same.
Through the years, you might say,
I've been counting up from ten,
For every year I've lost,
another year begins.

THE THIRD GENERATION

The tree I climbed in my front yard
still grows in wild expanse,
And the tree rings become faces that
I've come to know by chance.
Surrounded by my family on a summer-shortened day,
I need to tell them now before the
moments gone away.
Do they need me now as much as I need them?
Will they miss me when I'm gone and
we're counting down from ten?

I believe in what you are,
and what I make believe,
Is that walking closely by my side,
the worlds' answers up your sleeve.

I miss you in the morning when
I'm lying on my own,
While the ghosts of all the best years,
dance in fields being sown.

You've expressed and shared the excitement of this
day for decades,
And expect not to diminish the moment
for many more.

For underneath the paper, gifts, and photographs,
we came to know ourselves as a family.

There is nothing in the world
like Illinois rain.
Sparkling on the grass,
it will bring me home again.

Carol and Barbara

Harriet and Louis Jr. had two daughters, Carol and Barbara. Carol was born in 1934 and Barbara in 1937. They lived in a house on Greenview Avenue, which Louis later sold to his good friend, Buddy Ziehn, when they moved.

Carol recalls beginning to work at the store at an early age, just as her father had worked there as a boy. She and Barbara used to fold and stock gift boxes, and produce dozens of bows on a machine that they cranked to make the bows. There was another machine they cranked which produced long ribbons of price tags. They were supervised by their father or by Helen Lewerenz, who made sure all clothing was neatly ironed and had price tags.

As adolescents the girls "graduated" to work as sales clerks in the women's department, particularly lingerie and fabrics. Carol remembers the long laborious hours spent taking inventory in January of every bobbin of thread, every set of needles, every thimble, and every pair of shoe laces. This is all done by computers in a modern department store of today. She also remembers the strong cigars of Uncle Victor, which made her feel sick at times.

Carol tells a story about sister Barbara during World War II, when Barbara was about six-years-old. Leather and shoes were rationed at that time and a person was only allowed one pair of new shoes each year. A pretty pair of red shoes had caught Barbara's eyes and she insisted she had to have that pair of shoes, even though her father told her they were flimsy and would not hold up. A little girl's tears can melt a father's heart and he reluctantly bought the shoes to make her happy. A few weeks later Barbara wore the shoes in the rain and they got soaked. Soon after the leather straps began to deteriorate and break. The beautiful red shoes had to be thrown away and Barbara had to wear hand-me-down shoes the rest of the year.

THE THIRD GENERATION

Carol and Chuck Haggerty down on the farm in Canton.

Louis Jr. was an alumni of Knox College and Carol began attending there in 1952. Her major was English with a minor in education and she spent some time working as a substitute teacher as a young woman. She met a man in college named Chuck Haggerty and they were married in 1956. Chuck operated a successful pest extermination business in central Illinois and they settled in the small town of Canton. Chuck's hobbies were riding motorcycles and teaching his pet crow how to talk. They had two children, Andrea and Christian.

*Wedding day of Barbara and Gerry Weaver, 1959.
(left to right) Carol, Louis, Barbara, Harriet*

Barbara graduated as salutatorian of Maine Township High School in the class of 1955. Carol describes her as active and adventurous, and she learned to fly an airplane and water ski as a young woman. She majored in philosophy at Knox College and met a handsome and likeable young man there named Gerry Weaver whom she married in 1959. They had four children, Mark, David, Steven and Susan.

Gerry and Barbara lived in Des Plaines and Gerry managed the women's foundations, accessories, household goods and fabrics sections on the first floor. In 1975 he purchased a string of small dress shops in Ann Arbor, Michigan, and the family moved there so he could manage the stores.

CHAPTER 8

THE FAMILY COTTAGE

In the 1930's the three brothers, Victor, Walter and Louis Jr. purchased some property on the Fox River north of the county seat of McHenry. The river was less developed at the time and there were fewer motor boats and the fishing was good.

A small fishing shack the size of a room was built on the property for the purpose of shelter and storing fishing gear. This would later become a one-car garage for the cottage addition. There was no running water, but a hand pump was installed for that purpose outside the shack. There was electricity and a 1930's refrigerator which was a white enamel box on four legs with the motor and fan on top. It was installed in the shack to keep cleaned fish and cold beer. Bob states that there was an outhouse which he called a "two-holer" and occasionally someone threw a handful of lime in the hole to cut down on the odor. When the fishing was over for the day, one can imagine the brothers and their friends playing cards and having a drink. In modern parlance, this would be called a "man cave." Women were not invited.

After the Second World War the children of Victor, Walter and Louis Jr. had all become adults and were becoming married. Soon grandchildren were on the way. The three brothers realized that the fishing shack could never accommodate the needs of the expanded family, and so a simple wooden cottage was built on the property which was modern and even had a toilet that flushed. The cottage had two bedrooms, a living room, a small bathroom and kitchen, and a large screened-in porch. The fishing shack was converted to a one-car garage which was attached to the kitchen and continued to have the old refrigerator, some outboard motors, and fishing poles.

Front of cottage on Fox River, ca 1955.

The living room and one bedroom were in front of the cottage and were light and spacious. The bedroom was nicely decorated and our parents slept in this room. We three brothers slept on a full bed in the second bedroom in the middle of the house which had smaller windows and tended to have a musty smell. The sheets and blankets were cool and heavy as the river gave off a lot of moisture. I noticed that there was a cloth tag which was sewn on the mattress which had the name "Minnie Spiegler." I did not know who this was at the time, but I am glad no one told me that I was sleeping on the bed of my dead great-grandmother. It might have given me the willies.

THE FAMILY COTTAGE

* * *

Cousin Nancy writes, "As I was growing up (1950's – 1970's), it was our family's tradition to spend nearly every weekend in the summer at the family cottage on the Fox River. Visiting the cottage always meant boating, waterskiing and swimming in the river in back of the cottage. I loved to dig up the sand with my toes searching for clams. During the day, we would visit the old chapel at the Chapel Hill Golf Course. The chapel was very small and visits to this rather eerie place were brief for us kids. As night time came, we would plop into our Adirondack chairs to watch the boats with their lights as they cruised up and down the Fox River. My grandmother Pearl loved the cottage. She would sometimes arrive a couple days before us to relax and prepare for her grandchildren."

* * *

Roger holding two-foot long catfish, ca 1952.

Going Fishing

We did a lot of fishing at the river. By the time we were three or four, Dad would put a worm on the hook of our bamboo poles and we would go up and down the river fishing. We would walk the piers putting our bait in the cool shadows where the fish liked to lay. Once Glenn caught a catfish so big that it began pulling him into the water and Dad had to come to rescue him.

As we got older Dad took us on early morning fishing trips in a twelve-foot aluminum boat powered by an outboard motor. The bottom of the boat had many rivets and as the boat bounced over the waves the rivets would loosen and water would start coming into the bottom of the boat. We always had a couple of coffee cans in the boat to bail water and keep our feet dry. It was part of the ritual of fishing on the river. Every spring Dad would flip the boat over on dry land to expose the rivets and he would carefully glue or caulk them all, but after a month or two we were back to bailing.

We would put a large washtub in the boat and go under the Johnsburg Bridge, or into Dutch Creek, and the fishing was often very good. In a few hours we would have a hundred or more perch and bluegill in the washtub, and Dad felt this was enough.

Back on the front lawn of the cottage Dad would clean all those fish. When we were younger we just watched and kept him company. One thing I understood early on was that catching fish was more fun than cleaning and eating them.

As Dad would clean the fish, he would sing us songs, perhaps songs he learned from his father or in the Army. I noticed that he would never sing these songs when Mom was around. These were men songs, and only to be sung and shared with men. It was part of the ritual of boys spending time with their father.

> One of these songs went like this:
> Whiskey! Whiskey! Whiskey!
> It makes me feel so frisky!
> In the morn!
> In the corn!

Another song was longer with many verses and portrayed what happened to a person who had died in an auto accident. It begins by talking about the ambulance coming and the siren, but I no longer remember all of the verses. The verse which stood out in my mind was:

> The worms crawl in, the worms crawl out,
> the worms play pinochle in your snout.
> The pus it turns a deadly green
> And it all comes out like whipping cream.

You can understand why Mom would not like these songs. But for we boys, fishing and Dad's songs were good times.

Mary and Jay on pier, Bob with Ellayne holding Glenn in river, 1953.

The Cigar Store Indian

There were times Dad would take us fishing in Fox Lake or Grass Lake which were part of the waterways of the Chain of Lakes. We would take the boat and head north on the river until we got to Pistakee Bay, which is the southernmost body of water of the Chain. As we headed into the bay there was a store along the shoreline to the right where we would stop. The store was an old wooden building which was painted white and housed a bar, eating area, and a type of convenience store. We would stop there for soda pop and ice.

As we entered the large room of the establishment there was a long bar on the opposite wall and some small round tables with chairs in front of it. There was a clothed statue of a cigar store Indian which stood just inside the door as we entered. The Indian stood about seven-feet tall with a headdress on his head, a tan bare chest, and a loincloth around his waist.

The owner of the store was usually behind the bar cleaning glasses and preparing for the afternoon crowd. In the morning there were few people in the store. We were small boys at the time, and at some point the owner told us to lift up the back of the loincloth of the cigar store Indian. The owner had a smile on his face like a person who was about to set some catnip before three kittens.

We wondered why the owner wanted us to do this, but we went back to the Indian and carefully lifted up the loincloth covering his rear. Lo and Behold! A loud siren went off which startled us and we shouted. Dad and the owner were laughing, and soon we were laughing too. This was the most amazing thing we had seen in a long time.

Every few minutes or so we would go back to the Indian and lift up his loincloth and the siren would go off. We would shout and laugh and run around, and had the greatest time with this new discovery. I imagine eventually the adults got tired of hearing the siren and told us to knock it off. In the future, whenever we went into Pistakee Bay we always wanted to visit the Indian.

Matt Schulien

There was an elderly man named Matt Schulien who lived three cottages north of our cottage. He had a large, round stomach and a round, ruddy face with light curls of grey hair on top of his head. Mr. Schulien was so elderly and large that he drove around in a golf cart to visit others on the river. I never saw him walk.

Mr. Schulien was an owner of Schulien's Restaurant in Chicago, a well-known place which had been in business for decades. It served German cuisine, but the restaurant's claim-to-fame was that a magician came to each table to perform card and magic tricks while the people were sitting there and eating.

Mr. Schulien must have done this work when he was younger and healthier.

When we were young boys, Mr. Schulien used to drive his golf cart down to our cottage to see us. He would have a deck of cards, some coins, a handkerchief, and other items used to perform his tricks, and he would give us a private show. At age three or four, we were just the right audience, for we believed in magic. When Mr. Schulien pulled a card out from behind Glenn's ear, or found a coin in the waistband of his shorts, or had four aces up his sleeve, there was only one explanation. It had to be magic. We had never seen or known anyone who could do such impossible things. We were both amazed and amused at Mr. Schulien's tricks. For his part, Mr. Schulien probably got a kick out of our naive wonder and laughter.

Mr. Schulien was one of our favorite people. Whenever we arrived at the cottage, one of the first things we would do is walk to Mr. Schulien's cottage and see if he was out, but I never remember seeing him outside his house. We would go back to our cottage and play or fish, and eventually Mr. Schulien would come rolling along and we would gather round, and the magic would begin.

Spiegler store picnic at cottage, ca 1955. (left to right) Helen Lewerenz, Harriet Spiegler, and Fanny Sladik.

The Store Picnics

In the 1950's the store held a picnic at the cottage for its employees every summer. The three brothers always had a close relationship with the employees, and the picnics gave the opportunity for the store to come together on a social occasion. Pearl, Fanny, and Helen would come up to the cottage the day before to prepare the potato salad, baked beans, cole slaw, and set everything up.

There was a young woman who worked at the store who was Hungarian, and she and her extended family were a professional acrobatic and gymnastic troupe. They would come in costume to the cottage and set up a trampoline, high bar, and tumbling mats, and have a variety of balls and hoops to juggle. Their performance was one of the high points of the picnic; it was truly special.

We children liked to spend time in the river, jumping off the pier, swimming, and floating in the inner tubes. The elderly women would be sitting on lawn chairs on the banks watching us and chatting. Bob would take interested parties for rides in his speed boat and Grandpa (Walter) asked Mr. Schulien to come down to do card tricks. There was plenty of food for everyone and Fanny would come around with a tray of her delicious kolaches. Everyone appeared to enjoy these picnics a great deal.

Carol says that she asked Fanny for her kolache recipe several times, but Fanny would never share it with her. It was top secret. I suppose the recipe came from Fanny's days in Vienna when her family were the court florists for the Emperor. So with the death of Fanny and the royal baker, one of the most delicious kolache recipes in the world was lost forever.

Fox River Memories

It was a blue jay kind of day.

Flying overhead, their shrill cries pierced the air,

and the sun shone on a deep blue sky,

the warmth of its rays competing with the cold of the earth.

The wondrous smell of bacon being fried

wafted down the hallway,

a mother's way of telling her children

it was time to get up.

The floor felt cold and the air was cool,

but by noon we would go swimming

in the brown-green water

and fish with a bamboo pole under the piers.

We climbed the stile and fed grass to the cows,

and when Dad came home, we would ride in the boat.

All was right in the world.

It was a blue jay kind of day.

Jay

CHAPTER 9

COMMENTS FROM THE PEANUT GALLERY: THE FOURTH GENERATION

*Fourth generation grandchildren, 1956.
(left to right) Kurt, Glen, Jay, Tracy in front,
Jake, Rick with Walter in rear.*

These reflections and stories come from a period of time between 1956 and 1972, with contributions by Gail, her daughter Karla, Nancy and Susan.

Mannequins in the Front Window

When Glenn and I were small boys, about age four or five, Dad (Roger) used to take us to the store some Sunday mornings in order to change the apparel on the mannequins in the front window of the men's department. This was done periodically to reflect the clothing of the season and new fashions, and was just one of the eternal tasks of running a department store. As Dad went back and forth from the front window to the interior of the store putting away old apparel and getting new clothes for the mannequins to wear, Glenn and I would climb in the window to inspect the mannequins and play. If we spied a passerby walking down the sidewalk approaching the store, we would freeze into a rigid position wondering if the passerby would think we were just one of the mannequins. We would keep our eye on the person and see if they reacted. Somehow, I don't think we fooled anyone.

Fanny

There was an elderly lady named Fanny Sladik who worked in the fabrics section and she was always special to us. She had worked in the store for several decades, until she was in her nineties, and she was one of those people at the store who never seemed to change in her physical appearance or character in the twenty years I knew her. She was short and very thin, with a ball of salt and pepper grey hair around her face which was very wrinkled. She wore wire rim granny glasses and generally rouged her cheeks due to her light complexion. Even though she was very elderly, she was very spry and physically agile and her mind was sharp as a tack.

Roger said that her family had been the court florist for Emperor Franz Josef of the Austro-Hungarian Empire and that she spoke five languages. She was Hungarian by birth, but in this polyglot empire it was common to know several languages to communicate with everyone.

Fanny loved to make a fuss over us when we came in the store as she loved children. Dad would generally leave us and Fanny would take us to her locker in the basement where she kept a box of Tootsie Roll Pops on the top shelf. We had our choice of grape, orange or cherry. We knew Fanny loved us, and we considered her as another grandmother and always gave her a kiss when we saw her.

The Crumbling Wall

After the store was rebuilt, Louis Sr. eventually had a brick building with a basement built on the east side of the store. Bob says that this long narrow space which became the men's department was originally a barber shop which became a part of the store in the 1920's.

The brick basement section probably had a water problem, as the center of the floor was gravel. A narrow cement catwalk went around the gravel, hugging the brick walls. There were few shelves in this basement addition and most of the stock was on rolling racks which could be quickly removed in case of flooding. There was a single bay of fluorescent lights which ran down the center of this basement section and the lighting was so dim I had a hard time making out the walls on either side.

As you walked into the entrance way of this basement section there was a long, sturdy, wooden table against the opposite wall. There was an old-time scale with two brass pans sitting on this table with lead weights of various sizes, such as a half-pound, one pound, etc. Grandpa (Walter) used the scale to weigh packages he wanted to mail so he could affix accurate postage. As small children we would go in this section and play with the scale and weights.

What was unusual about this setup was that the brick wall behind the table was slowly crumbling and becoming a pile of dirt. The pile of dirt was not small; it was several feet long and a foot high. For thirty years or longer, no one had ever swept up that pile of crumbling dirt. It always struck me as ironic that upstairs was a light, modern, clean store and downstairs in the basement this brick wall was just allowed to crumble.

Taking Inventory

When Glenn and I entered middle school, Dad (Roger) asked us to work at the store to take inventory. Taking inventory was an annual event at the store which occurred the first ten days of the new year. All the stock in the store, which was several million items, had to be counted with their wholesale price to know the value of all the merchandise which had not been sold and whether the store had made any profit that year. The profit was divided up among the owners in the family.

On the price tag of each item of the merchandise was not only the retail price, but the wholesale price was written in code letters. Each price tag had 3-5 code letters, which the customer did not understand. The code word used to understand the code was "CHAMBERPOT", each letter standing for one of the first ten numerals. Whoever chose this code word, and I think it went back a ways, obviously enjoyed bathroom humor or just humor in general.

Dad, David, Howard, or others would go through each item of merchandise and call out the code letters, and Glenn and I would sit at the folding card table and put a hash mark after each group of code letters. For one type of item, such as men's suits, we might have a list of 20-30 groups of code letters, each representing a wholesale price, in front of us. We would spend hours just sitting at the card tables and making these hash marks, a very tedious job. It was not fun, and we were not paid, but we did it because we were members of the family.

One man who did the calling to us was Bob Meuhlenbeck. He owned a landscaping company, but in the winter there was no work due to the cold and snow, and so he worked at the store. He was about forty years of age with dark hair cut in a crewcut, a well-tanned face, and glasses with thick black plastic frames. What was unique about Bob was that he had the personality and zany sense of humor reminiscent of the comedian Jerry Lewis. He was always joking, and nothing was sacred. As he had a captive audience in Glenn and I and the work was so boring, it gave him the perfect opportunity to cut up and make the work go faster. He would make jokes about the merchandise, the salesclerks, and us. He was the only person I knew who would poke fun at the Spieglers. Sometimes Dad would be around and listen in, and he would just smile. He was just glad the work was being done.

Spiegler staff, Des Plaines "Frontier Days," 1953.

Reflections by Karla

When I was approximately six and seven, I believe my father (David) thought it would be reasonable to bring me to the store on occasional Saturdays. It was time to expose me to some structure and actually work. In total, I worked part-time and full time for Spiegler's until I was nineteen-years-old.

My youngest years remember simply being awe-struck with the size of the store, the beautiful and different items on display, and all of lines and lines of inventory; not only items in full view on the main two floors, but especially items found in the basement. These early years were mostly spent in this basement of the store. (Likely the years of six to ten+.)

What an incredibly, amazing, huuuge basement! What an incredibly interesting place! It was a labyrinth of aisles, of dark tones, overhead plumbing, electricity lines, and miles of cement and piles and piles of clothing – on ever-reaching wooden shelving.

Those low ceilinged aisles were illuminated by only bare, long fluorescent light tubes. There were two basements, and the second basement was one a young girl such as myself took dares to walk into. The second basement would be entered via a small cement up-ramp, and the tall men sometimes had to remember to duck their heads to get through the door frame. Usually, on the right of the up-ramp, the store shelved the tops and bottoms of gift boxes.

The main basement room was filled with, seemingly, many working tables. One, an old ping-pong table, another, a square Formica table, which would fit four people, but at the lunch hour we would sometimes squeeze around the corners five, six or more. Multiple copies of the local newspaper were always around, the sections separated by mid-morning, ending in several sections around the entire room. The Formica table would be swept clean for a number of other activities. While primarily it was our lunch table, in the evenings the men gathered, had a drink, a cigarette, a pipe, and maybe played a bit of cards.

However! It was the top of this Formica table, okay and sometimes the edge of the ping-pong table, where I was taught my first most important job! It was the construction of bows destined for gift boxes! To make this bow it took a gun-silver metal, heavy, square, piece of machinery. I was taught to set a 'button' into the machinery's special slot, choose my ribbon color from a wide array of choices, hook the first loop of ribbon in its place, and THEN with exactly twelve circular hand cranked turns, I had a wonderful and pretty bow! It remained an amazing piece of machinery to me. Usually, one would see Helen or Fanny at this machine, but just sometimes it got to be me. The second most very important task was to set up the tops and bottoms of gift boxes. From a long wooden work table near the

Formica table, or on the Formica table, I would place box bottoms to the left of me, and box tops to the right of me. THEN I would commence the 'construction' of tops with bottoms.

I especially remember Louis, Grandpa, sometimes, Bob, Roger or Dad working on taking goods in and marking the shipping receipts properly. They were making certain every item from its box was accounted for. Inventory arrived at the street level, off-loaded from this skinny alley where a big truck parked. Boxes of goodies were sent whizzing down the 'cellar' stairwell on a wooden ramp. The ramp was slick from so many years of box sliding and had an (albeit-dirty) sheen to it and I often wished I could take myself for a ride.

My primary experiences centered on the dry goods, jewelry, infant, adolescent, Girl Scout, and foundation departments. The men's department was another territory. I was always a part and yet not. Being a 'girl' I never felt 'allowed' to mingle too long. On that 'side,' Vi was our only female employee and a great men's department employee for years. To my eyes, she held a special role, and was to be fully respected, and a delight to befriend. Spiegler employees were always very, very, friendly, very nice people. They smiled a lot, sometimes shared food they cooked from home.

Dad, (Dave) Roger or Bob would ask them to help set up the front of the store's window displays. This was always another amazing space to spend time in. Here I thought I could see the rest of the world from these windows, and the irony of life (facetiously and later realized) . . . we were on display for the world to see. What interesting work it seemed to be to move mannequins, dismantle mannequins (nearly human!), and dress and undress them. We could add fake fall leaves, set up lights, and add sprigs of trees with spring buds around them.

More on life in the store's basement. There were two other highly utilized corners of the basement. The bathrooms (one men's and one women's). These rooms reminded me of something found in cabins, and I was always fascinated with the high raised tank with a chain flush. How old! Then there was the 'kitchen'. Hmmm. A deep utility sink, a couple or more shelves, and counter . . . I seem to recall. Lots of coffee cups, odds and ends of plates, utensils, etc. Even at the tender ages of something between six and ten did I think the place needed a real scrubbing! However, sometimes we would find doughnuts and coffee cakes and pastries waiting for us there. All of this thanks to the wonderful employees that baked at home.

Spiegler store with new facade, ca 1961

Reflections by Nancy

These are memories of Nancy, the oldest child of Bob and Mary Spiegler.

The store holds many memories for me. As a child, I would play hide-and-seek with my younger sister, Susan, in the back basement which still had a mud floor from the original store. There were many rows of wood shelves built by Bob; the shelves spanned the complete length of the store above and contained a huge amount of inventory. Walter's son, David, oversaw the company's advertising and signage. I recall watching Uncle David in the basement as he manually set the metal type in wood trays and then rolled ink over the type; he then used another roller to make signs for sales and special promotions. I was always amazed at the number of signs that were required for special sales. Other memories include taking inventory in the notions department which included the painstaking task of counting each individual needle that was housed in tiny wood containers. During Halloween, across from the notion department, many costumes were featured in boxes which always contained a mask and costume. At Christmas time, the area was used to provide a selection of toys for the customers. Spiegler's was one of the only places to shop for years. I was told years before my time this area was where the grocery counter and crank-style register were, along with barrels of flour.

When I was still a child, the second floor became a retail area. In keeping with community traditions at the time, the store was closed on Sunday but we would go there after church to try on and buy school clothes for the next season. For many years, the store was the local provider of all Boy Scout and Girl Scout supplies, uniforms and gifts. Ladies apparel and Girl Scouts plus the store office and buying office were on the second floor.

If A Store Could Talk... The Spiegler Family Remembers

I worked at Spieglers for nine years, starting by making bows in the basement with Grandma Pearl when I was age thirteen. It was store policy to offer to gift wrap all purchases. When I was older and working in sales, I became a great package wrapper! By age sixteen I was assistant buyer for lingerie; by eighteen, was giftware and jewelry buyer. I met my husband, Gary, when I was there working during Christmas break of my senior year in college. In the late 1980's the family moved the store into the Des Plaines mall. Husband Gary and many of his teacher friends plus family assisted one weekend with moving the entire store into the new facility. Moving back and forth between buildings with rack after rack of clothing was quite the spectacle and an amazing feat!

Spiegler's Department Store was the nucleus of the family and its employees were treated like family. The employees were the heart of the business and many worked well past retirement age. Each year the store would host two very popular parties. The annual Christmas party was a fabulous event of food and celebration. The party began as soon as the doors closed and went into the night. The other party was the annual picnic, held at the family-owned cottage in Fox Lake. There was food, of course, and entertainment including trapeze artists and magicians. Matt Schulien lived next door to the Spiegler cottage and he loved to do card tricks for the children. In 1886, his family built a famous old-world German restaurant called Schulien's. His son, Charlie, was the last of three generations to operate the restaurant which was located on Irving Park Road in Chicago and closed in 1999.

Spiegler men, ca 1970. (left to right) Bob, Dave, Roger, Walter, Louis

The Dollar Table

The Dog Days of summer came in July. It was hot and humid outside, and customers in the store were scarce. Everyone had bought their summer wardrobe of swimsuits and shorts and were off on vacation, and the back-to-school traffic would not begin until mid-August. In order to draw customers into the store, a big summer sale was held in July and the featured event in the men's department was the Dollar Table. When Glenn and I turned sixteen, we became salesclerks and participants in the sale.

The Dollar Table was a folding card table on which Dad (Roger) piled all sorts of items which were not selling well. They might have undesirable colors or stylistic features or be out of fashion like Nehru shirts and bell bottoms.

Besides these "dogs", Dad would add some items of higher value just so the women shoppers would know there were some real bargains on the table. The table was piled high with bargains, and everything was a dollar.

Even though the Dollar Table was in the men's department and sold male clothing, no men ever came to the event. It was always women who loved shopping and bargains. On the day of the event there would be a crowd of women waiting outside the front door for the store to open. Once the doors were open, they came in like a swarm of bees and soon there was a mob at the Dollar Table. One thing I quickly learned, you do not want to be standing between that table and the crowd of women. It would definitely be dangerous. We salesclerks waited safely behind the counter by the cash register, watching the scene and waiting to ring up the sales.

The women near the table were holding up items in the air, examining them, discussing the items with their friends, and sometimes throwing the items back on the table. The women at the rear of the crowd were jostling so they could get up to the bargains. Finally the women at the table would have their prized bargains and come to us to be rung up, and other women would take their place around the table. After a few hours the Dollar Table had been picked pretty clean and customers had been drawn into the store to buy other things.

The Junkman

After the July summer sale was over, an elderly man with grey hair came to the store from Chicago who Dad (Roger) called the "Junkman." I believe he may have been Jewish. He owned a store in Chicago, probably off Maxwell Street south of the Loop, an area known for bargains, and he bought all the merchandise in the store which the owners wanted to get rid of. This might be items which were considered out of fashion, but also clothing with flaws such as a stain mark from a pin, a hole in the fabric, a chip in a mirror, or fading caused by being on a mannequin in the front window. All of these items were basically unsalable. Dad knew that, and the Junkman knew that. Dad would pile all such items on a counter and the Junkman would offer him a single price for the whole lot. Dad and the Junkman would haggle a bit, each man knowing the position of the other, and they would settle on a price. It was a mutually beneficial relationship, as it at least gave the store some money for unsalable items, and the Junkman could somehow get the customers in Chicago to buy the merchandise at a higher price than he paid.

As the Junkman came all the way from Chicago, he was in no rush to return. He and Dad would joke for awhile. The Junkman would tell some jokes he had come across in his travels, and they both seemed to enjoy the time and appreciate the relationship. I do not remember any of the jokes unfortunately.

The Basement Men's Bathroom

The main basement to the store was dug in the second decade of the twentieth century and at some time in the 1920's the town probably had developed a municipal water and sewage system and a male and female bathroom were put into the basement. These tiny bathrooms were up against a brick exterior wall behind the marking table where Helen Lewerenz sat at her sewing machine. The women's bathroom was behind the men's bathroom and there was a narrow passageway lined with tongue-in-groove ribbed wood which connected to the two bathrooms. At some point in time all the wood paneling had been painted gloss enamel powder blue. To say it was archaic would have been an understatement.

The men's bathroom had a single toilet set on a concrete floor with the wood paneling and a light overhead. I believe there was a small sink in the corner. The bathroom was so small and barren that it reminded us of an outhouse. The only difference was that the toilet flushed. I do not know the condition of the women's bathroom, but the female employees generally used the modern, spacious, clean facilities on the second floor.

There was a stock boy named Jim Kelly who had a sense of humor. One day he brought some yellow paint and painted a crescent moon on the outside of the powder blue door to the men's bathroom, reminiscent of an outhouse. He felt it matched the decor. We all smiled when we saw this, but didn't say anything. At some point in time Walter and Louis, who always worked in the basement, must have seen this, but never had the moon removed. It just seemed to fit.

Bud Barrett

An older man named Bud Barrett came to work in the men's department about the same time I did. He was a retired businessman and wanted to work part-time to pass the time and earn some money.

Bud had grey hair which was cut in a short crewcut. He tended to be serious and frank, and did not tolerate any nonsense. I believe he was a former Marine, and they say "once a Marine, always a Marine."

Despite his gruffness at times, we got along very well and he took me under his wing. When I would come in on a Thursday evening or Saturday to work, he would announce, "The First Team is here," which meant we would be working together.

After the summer sale was over at the store, things got very slow for several weeks. As there were no customers, Bud and I would stand by the front window and chat, watching people walk up and down the sidewalks and getting off the Chicago and Northwestern train. Sometimes as I was gazing across the railroad tracks, Bud would spy a woman walking down the sidewalk towards us. He would nudge me or motion with his eyes and say, "What do you think of this one?"

As I was only sixteen and any adult woman I associated with my mother, I would invariably say, "She's too old."

And Bud would always reply, "There's nothing like dealing with an old established firm."

The Steam Pipe

The stockroom downstairs took up about two-thirds of the main basement room. It consisted of four aisles running lengthwise down the basement with wooden shelves made of planks. The whole stockroom was on a raised eight-foot pedestal or riser, which indicated there may have been a water problem at one time.

A ten-inch cast iron steam pipe ran down the center aisle of the stockroom. It was to carry steam from a coal furnace and boiler to radiators on the two floors of the store, but had not been used in two decades once the store converted to natural gas and a forced air heating system. Like some of the other relics of a by-gone era which existed in the basement, it was never removed as no customers ever saw it.

As a salesman for the men's department, I might go into the stockroom ten to twenty times a day to fetch merchandise of the desired size and color for a customer. It was just a fact of life, as the showroom upstairs was never large enough to hold all the stock. Each time I went into the stockroom, I would have to duck my head slightly to avoid hitting that steam pipe. I was in the stockroom so many times it was just second nature to duck. But once in a great while, I would be thinking more about the merchandise I wanted to get for the customer, and I'd forget about the steam pipe. I'd be walking briskly down the short aisle which was perpendicular to the steam pipe and WHAM! My forehead would smash right into it. It was like someone hitting me on the head with a hammer. I'd see stars and my head would start hurting. Even though I had an awful headache, I knew I had a customer waiting upstairs so I would always keep going to get the merchandise and worry about the headache later.

Timeless Quality of the Store

There was a timeless quality about the old store whenever I was there. Whether I was five or twenty-five-years-old, very little seemed to change. The physical plant, the people, where they were stationed and what they did, remained the same. Although it seems peculiar to me as I look back at it now, when I was there it seemed perfectly normal.

Many of the staff, both the Spieglers and the regular employees, worked there for decades. They worked in the same department, and did the same tasks, year after year. Grandpa and Louis were always at the counter at the back of the basement doing shipping and receiving merchandise, and Helen was at her sewing machine. Fanny was always in fabrics, Winnie Congdon in foundations, and Arlene up front with the purses and jewelry. Margaret, Grace and some other older ladies were in the women's department, Dorothy Mills was the office manager upstairs, and Dad (Roger), David, Howard Richardson and Vi Kleckner were in the men's department. No one ever had to tell staff how to do their jobs, or oversee them, as they had been doing the work for so long. They could tell the Spieglers how to do it, and sometimes did.

To add to this vision of timelessness, it always seemed to me as a boy growing up that some people never even changed in physical appearance. Fanny and Winnie were always elderly, grey-haired ladies and Vi was always smartly dressed in perfect style in the men's department. Dad, David, Howard or Bob never greyed or changed their hairstyle and always looked much the same.

Des Plaines Journal, May 20, 1965

Helen Lewerenz was a heavy-set elderly woman who was the store seamstress and had her sewing machine in the basement. She always had white hair in soft curls, granny glasses, and wore an apron over a loose-fitting Mother Hubbard dress. Her ancient Singer sewing machine had a treadle board to power it, but at some time an electric motor had been jerry-rigged to move the bobbin more quickly. Helen and her sewing machine sat in the same spot on the marking table for twenty years, her back to the men's room. When not sewing, she put price tags on the new merchandise which lay on the marking table. Helen, the furniture, her tasks, never changed.

Walter and Louis would take a break in the middle of each morning to go for coffee at the Mandas Diner on the corner of Lee and Ellinwood. They met several of their old buddies like Tat Kennicott or True Wilson there. It was their routine and they did it day after day, year after year.

As everyone worked together for so long and knew each other well, the store as a whole was a type of caring family. The line between the Spiegler family and the rest of the employees was blurred, on an emotional level. When I was in the store as a boy and young man, I always interacted with people as if they were extended family, and they did the same with me. At times family members of employees would show up and add to the mix. It was more than a place where people punched a time clock for eight hours to get a salary; people wanted to be there and felt good about each other. When Victor died, Walter became the benevolent father figure who looked out for everyone, and people looked out for him. A business which was run by family was actually a business that was a family.

Jay and Glenn with Helen at the marking table, 1956.

Reflections by Gail

These comments by Gail sent to me in a letter give a fuller picture of the store and its employees. Gail worked at the store and married David Spiegler and her mother, Grace Leyns, also worked in the women's department.

I faintly remember the grocery department. (I also remember David delivering groceries to my grandmother. I thought he was cute. I was probably eleven and David sixteen.) I remember the basement office, ping-pong/marking table, the pull chain flush toilet, the freight elevator and the second basement where David would sometimes sneak a nap on the overalls after a hard night. Around the holidays, Spiegler's was noted for serving greetings and refreshments to well- known Des Plainesites. The basement was also the scene of the employee Christmas party. Great fun and lots of refreshments for everyone.

But the store was its employees. Fanny Sladik was loved and disliked by many. She could and would sell anything, but was sometimes too pushy. Winnie Congdon was the foundations lady. Loretta Eck, Margaret Smith, Debbie Newhall,

Ruth Mahler, Grace Leyns, my mother, loved doing the fashion shows, Dorothy Butenschoen, the Girl Scout lady, and Edna Federwitz in the notions department. They were all headed up by Bob and for a time, Gerry Weaver.

The office had wonderful, patient Dorothy Mills. Betty Anderson, who loved working for Spiegler's, once said that she had so much fun, she felt that she should pay Spiegler's to work there. Also Karla Peterson, all headed up by Louis.

It sure is a wonder that the five Spiegler men and Pearl got along for so many years. I think it was a happy place to work, serving the community until progress got in the way. We never became Marshall Field's, Belk's, or J.C. Penney, but we had a good run and landed on our feet. What more can you ask!

Memories by Susan

Susan was the second child of Bob and Mary Spiegler. Some of her thoughts are recorded here.

I have such fond memories of the store, here are just a few.

As a child in the original Spiegler's Department Store I remember playing in the basement with school friends and drinking Fanta grape soda! I was always excited when we would get in new shipments of stuffed animals, hoping my grandma would give me one for Christmas! (She always did.)

It was fun to help my grandmother (Pearl) make bows on the bow machine, or print up little price tickets and attach them to new incoming goods. My sister and I enjoyed playing hide-and-seek between the many rows and boxes of inventory.

I worked part-time through high school in the summers and during Christmas. Spiegler's offered free wrapping which created a 'sharp' learning curve when you are young. Wrapping the giftware cube boxes were the hardest to master.

Speaking of Christmas, who could forget that Santa's house was located directly across from Spieglers on the opposite side of Ellinwood Street! I'm convinced to this day that Des Plaines had the REAL SANTA! My sister Nancy and I had our pictures taken with Santa several times for the local newspapers.

After college, I decided to work with my dad (Robert) for a few years in the new store. I ended up staying for the next seven years until we sold the store. We had the best time co-managing the entire women's floor. I loved helping Dad set up huge sales for our customers and creating fabulous fashion and cosmetic displays. Several times a month we would go to the Chicago Apparel Center where we would buy the latest trends in lady's fashion, jewelry and accessories. Dad would always negotiate for the best possible prices so we could in turn pass those savings on to our customers.

At the start of every day before opening the doors, Dad would cheer on our sales associates saying, "What are we going to do today?" and they would all cheerfully respond back saying, "sell, sell, sell!" We had the best employees and they were truly part of our family. We had one employee named Fanny who worked into her 90's just because she wanted too. Everyone who knew her just loved Fanny.

Just south of the railroad tracks on River Road there is a memorial boulder given by the Lions club in remembrance of my grandfather Vic. He was a community and civic leader in Des Plaines. I was only a baby when he died, and although I never met him, I still think of him every time I drive by.

Community service has always been important to the Spiegler family. One of my most treasured memories was entertaining the troops at Great Lakes

Naval Base for the Miss America Organization. After being runner-up to Miss Illinois Teenager twice and competing in the Miss Illinois Pageant as Miss York Township 1977 (Miss America) I decided to 'give back' by holding a Miss Des Plaines Pageant to compete at the Miss Illinois Pageant in the 1980's. We were only given the opportunity for one year due to a pageant license maximum, but everyone enjoyed the entire experience. The contestants had fun representing Spieglers in a mall fashion show open to the public and we gave them all make-up tips in our cosmetic department. It was an honor helping these young ladies gain self confidence to pursue their dreams, share their personal platforms, and help serve their community.

The Sand Blaster

One day a young man walked into the men's department in a pair of khaki pants and a white T-shirt which were heavily soiled. I greeted him and he said he was working on a scaffold sand-blasting the stone facade of the Des Plaines National Bank and needed a new pair of pants, so I took him back to the pants section. I got a tape measure and went down on one knee to measure the inseam of his pants. I placed one end of the tape measure on the top of his shoe and slowly unrolled the tape measure upward. Once the tape got up to his crotch, I could see he had a large hole in his pants there and he was not wearing underwear and his privates were exposed. Yeah, this guy needed a pair of pants bad! I decided it was best not to act surprised or flustered, and so I got up and measured his waist, and told him I had some nice Dickies work pants downstairs in his size. I asked him to give me a few minutes while I brought up some pants in different colors.

Once I had brought the work pants upstairs, he selected one pair and tried it on in the dressing room and said he liked them. He removed his belt and wallet from the old pair of pants and put them on his new pair and said he would wear them out of the store. Once he had paid for his new pants, he told me I could dispose of the old ones, and he walked out the door to continue his sandblasting. Yes, I had done my part to protect Des Plaines from indecent exposure that day.

The World War I Veteran

One day an elderly man came into the men's department and made a small purchase, like a pair of stockings. He was about Grandpa's (Walter) age and was probably a friend of his. As I stood behind the counter and was preparing to ring up the sale, the man began reminiscing and talking about his experience as a soldier in World War I. I was interested in what he had to say, as I had never met a World War I veteran before, and I try to be a good listener.

The old gentleman must have had a need to talk about his war experience and the battles in which he fought, as he talked a long time that day. At one point he pulled up his trousers on one leg and showed me where a German canister of mustard gas had exploded and wounded him. Eventually Dad came up and he shared his experiences fighting in Europe during the Second World War, and the two reminisced together.

One thing that struck me after this conversation was that the store was about more than selling pieces of merchandise. It was about relationships. In fact, the relationships were probably more important in the continuance of the store than the merchandise it sold. Thousands of people from the community came in each year to buy clothing, year after year, and they had formed relationships and friendships with all the people who worked at the store. They trusted that they would get good quality merchandise at a fair price, and they also felt that the salesclerks knew them and cared about them. There was a connection.

When people go into a large department store or warehouse outlet today, they generally know no one there. The modern customer ranges from store to store looking for the merchandise they want at the lowest price. It is often rare to find a salesclerk in such stores, and if you see one, they generally are not interested in waiting on you. The managers are rarely around, and certainly no one is interested in talking a long time with you. The personal connection is missing. Even though we may find the merchandise we want and get a good price, the aspect of personal relationships and sense of community is missing, and this is a real loss.

The Returned Shirt

One day a man came into the men's department and pulled a shirt out of a brown paper bag. He explained that he bought the shirt here and wanted to exchange it. I asked him if he had the receipt or the original wrapping for the shirt, but he had nothing. In looking at the wrinkled shirt, I could tell it had probably been worn and washed a number of times, and might be a few years old. I thought the man was pulling a fast one and I felt like telling him that we would not exchange the shirt, but I decided that before I said anything, I better check with Dad (Roger).

I found Dad in the back of the store and I showed him the worn shirt and explained the situation to him. Dad looked at the shirt a few seconds and then said, "Let the man pick out a new shirt." so I went back to the man and told him he could exchange the shirt for something comparable in price and that's what he did.

Dad understood that it was worth it to lose a few dollars on a new shirt rather than lose a good customer who might spend thousands of dollars at the store in his lifetime. Each customer was valuable, as they were the lifeblood of the store. In a small town business, the customer was always right because we wanted to maintain a positive relationship with the person and keep them coming back.

Walter Morava's Store

A man named Walter Morava operated a small shop next to the Des Plaines National Bank where he sold stationery and tobacco products. Although this would be considered an unusual combination today, Mr. Morava stayed in business over twenty years with it.

Mr. Morava was a neat, dapper man and it always struck me that he was very European in his appearance. He would generally wear dress pants and a white shirt with a tie and nice vest as opposed to a suit coat. His straight dark hair was parted and combed over to one side and he had a shaving brush mustache under his nose. He was the only man I ever knew who had a mustache like that other than Adolf Hitler.

When Glenn and I were young boys we wanted to buy our grandfathers a present every Christmas, and Dad would take us to Mr. Morava's shop to buy something. Grandpa Spiegler smoked a pipe and Grandpa Partridge smoked cigars, so we always bought them some. In the late 1950's and early 1960's no one ever said that tobacco was dangerous for a person's health. Little did we know that our presents may have hastened our grandfathers towards their eternal home.

As a boy, I came to understand that there was an informal system whereby the merchants supported each other socially and economically. They knew each other well because they met each other frequently at the Chamber of Commerce, the Lions Club or the Elks Club, or church. Each merchant made a point of shopping at other merchants' stores as part of this support network and as children we came to know a number of businessmen because we met them in their stores and they and their families would come to our home to socialize. We bought stationery from Mr. Morava, an Oldsmobile from Don Ladendorf, appliances from Johnny Alonge behind the movie theatre, sporting goods at Johnson's, and we took our clothes to Burchard's Dry Cleaning to be cleaned. Even when we moved to Mt. Prospect, we always shopped in Des Plaines. It was our community.

CHAPTER 10

THE DES PLAINES MALL

The 1960's and 1970's were a time of great prosperity and optimism for the United States. America was the wealthiest and most powerful country in the world and the goods produced by American manufacturing were valued and bought by people all over the globe. Science and technology were making great strides in improving the quality of life, and dreaded diseases such as smallpox and polio were being eradicated. The middle class continued to grow and real wages increased with the help of labor unions. Americans continued their romance with the automobile with gasoline costing 25 cents a gallon and President Dwight D. Eisenhower, commander of Allied forces in Europe during World War II, had initiated an ambitious program for a national interstate highway system modeled after the German autobahn. President John F. Kennedy, with the assistance of captured Nazi rocket scientist Werner von Braun, had declared that the United States would begin a space program to place an American on the moon. Business entrepreneurs sought to capitalize on the climate of optimism and prosperity and set about to create what was to become the great mecca of the American shopper, the enclosed indoor shopping mall.

The indoor shopping mall was a unique creation which was designed to capture a good portion of the money which Americans wanted to spend. It was intended to reduplicate and replace the downtown business district of nearby towns, while offering distinct advantages. Generally, one or more large national chain department stores were the financial anchors of the mall, and then there were a multitude of smaller specialty stores. In most malls you could find the same goods and services provided by a downtown business district, often at lower prices. There were boutiques and apparel stores, hair salons, shoe repair shops, restaurants, and even a movie theatre.

And to lure shoppers into the mall, various entertainers were often brought in to perform. At Christmas time there were lights and the traditional decorations, and the mall presented almost a carnival-like atmosphere. In many places the mall became the new psychological heart of the community, where senior citizens strolled for exercise and teenagers hung out to be cool.

Business people from the traditional commercial districts across the country were very concerned that these large indoor malls would draw away a significant portion of their business, and the northwest suburbs and Des Plaines were no exception in sharing this concern. The Golf Mill and Old Orchard Shopping centers had been built in Skokie and Niles to the east, Randhurst to the northwest, and Woodfield Mall, the grand-daddy of all shopping malls, was being planned in Schaumburg. In the mid-1960's businessmen and city officials in Des Plaines formed a not-for-profit study group and with the assistance of outside consultants looked at the feasibility of various types of urban redevelopment.

The study group met for years, and looked at every model from simply giving existing buildings a more attractive facelift to blocking off some streets to car traffic and re-paving the street with brick or cobblestones to give the business district an "old-timey" nostalgic look. Ultimately the plan which the study group put forward was an ambitious one, the creation of a whole new indoor mall to rival the other malls in the area. Urban planners recommended a "mixed-use" plan where office space, condominium towers for residents, and the shopping mall would all be close together. The idea was that many people would live, work, and shop in the same locale, the business district, and save money in not motoring to shopping malls. In a sense, this model went back to an earlier era of America when villages and small towns were the compact places where people lived and shopped.

In the end the study group recommended an enclosed mall be built on the block currently occupied by the Spiegler store and parking lot. The Spiegler family already owned a substantial portion of the land on the block. After much discussion the Spiegler family, the business community, and the city decided to accept the plan. A three-story enclosed mall with an interior courtyard was built with the Spiegler store occupying all three levels at one end of the mall and specialty shops in the remainder of the mall. A ten-story office building was built on the corner of Lee and Prairie Streets with the First National Bank of Des Plaines occupying the first three stories. The city, under the leadership of Mayor Herbert Behrel issued bonds to construct a three-level concrete parking garage which ran parallel to the railroad tracks between the mall and the train station. The city was concerned if there was no type of urban renewal for the downtown, businesses would slowly close and the city would lose tax revenues. The planning group even envisioned a future expansion of the block with condominiums and more shops which was dubbed "Superblock." The businesses facing Ellinwood Street remained open while the mall was constructed behind them and then demolished in the fall of 1977 when the mall was ready for occupancy.

Bank tower and Des Plaines Mall, 1978.

The store enjoyed good sales and profits for the first years in the mall. The regular customers continued to come and people who worked in the office tower or who were new to town came out of curiosity. But the mall itself had some problems at the outset which it was never able to resolve. One large problem was that the mall developer was unable to rent all the space in the mall and thus was unable to pay the $50,000 per month mortgage payment. Northwest Bank, which held the majority of the mortgage, called in the loan and the mall went into receivership. Eventually the developer was able to sell the mall to an investor named David Friedman and businessmen and public officials remained optimistic about the future.

Another problem was that the Behrel parking garage, an unadorned concrete structure, was viewed by some in the town as an eyesore. Many complained that the block-long structure had cut the downtown area in two. Merchants pointed out that people coming into the city from Northwest Highway and the north could not see and find the mall. The issue of the parking garage soured some public officials on the whole concept of an expanded Superblock.

Business remained good at the store until the recession of 1981-1983, when business sales and profits contracted across the nation. President Reagan had greatly expanded the armed forces through a series of tax increases while cutting federal expenditures on the backs of welfare recipients and the disabled who collected supplemental security income. The federal fiscal policy increased the depth and length of the recession. Ordinary citizens dealt with the recession by going in increasing numbers to the large malls and big box stores where they could get the cheapest prices for the goods they desired. Even after the recession was over, sales were never as robust as they had been at the Des Plaines mall. A great number of people had changed their shopping habits.

Interior of three-level mall.

The year of 1987 was a time of decision for the family, as their lease was due to expire in November and they would have to renew their lease for another ten years. Pearl had not worked at the store in years and Walter had retired at the age of eighty-six, gradually slipping into the night of Alzheimer's Disease. Louis Jr., Roger, Bob and David were at retirement age and had no strong desire to work another ten years.

Most of the fourth generation of the family had worked at the store as adolescents and young adults and had no interest in spending their lives selling clothing and household items other than perhaps Kurt, David's son, who had worked in the men's department for the past ten years. The fourth generation wanted to pursue different careers, see new parts of the globe, and rub elbows with new groups of people. The older generations did not resent them for this, as they had been raised to be intelligent and independent and follow their own star.

Ultimately the family decided not to renew the ten-year lease in the mall and the business was sold to the mall owner, David Friedman. Mr. Friedman hired a young lady to serve as store manager and Roger, Bob and David stayed on to help train her and insure continuity in the business. They gradually faded out of this role and went on to retire to more pleasant pursuits of golf, fishing and travel.

Business in the store continued to decline despite the best efforts of the manager. With the Spiegler family gone, the relationships with thousands of customers were also gone and many people stopped coming to the store and mall. Eventually less profitable sections of the store such as the children's department or Scouting were discontinued, but even this did not help.

The Christmas season is when most retail stores ring up the majority of their sales and show a profit for the year, but business at the Des Plaines Mall was dismal for the Christmas of 1991. The novelty of the place had worn off and most of the people shopping there were mall walkers or workers from the office tower. The mall had never achieved full vacancy. The owner of the mall was able to read the handwriting on the wall and so after Christmas he announced the closing of the store. A going-out-of-business sale was held and the store officially closed in March of 1992. With the closing of the anchor store of the mall, the owner was unable to make the mortgage payments and soon after declared bankruptcy. The mall was closed, to the disappointment of the business community and city officials. The city of Des Plaines was now stuck with a large vacant white elephant providing no tax revenues and the mall and parking garage were demolished less than twenty years after being constructed. Eventually condominium towers were built where the mall had stood and a new tall public library building now stands on Ellinwood Street where the old store had sat.

Although part of the failure of the Des Plaines Mall could be blamed on poor planning and over-enthusiasm on the part of city officials, in fact downtown malls created as part of urban renewal never did well across the United States. They were never able to successfully compete with the large indoor malls which offered a greater number of stores and goods at lower prices. Several Des Plaines Malls could have fit within Woodfield Mall in Schaumburg, which is indeed a large mall. And downtown malls were never able to eliminate the inconvenience to shoppers of fighting through congested traffic and easily finding free parking. There had been a fundamental shift in the shopping habits of the American consumer with the advent of these large malls and factors such as proximity, nostalgia, and civic pride were just not enough to lure them back on a regular basis.

Karla Jacobsen, who had served as business manager at the store for the last nineteen years after the retirement of Dorothy Mills, had said in a final interview on the closing of the store that it was "the end of an era." This was an accurate observation. It was the end of the era for the business which began as a general store, the Spiegler family, the city of Des Plaines, and actually thousands of towns and small cities across America. Due to changes in technology, the American consumer with an automobile was no longer tied to shopping in the nearby town business district. They could easily drive to an outlying mall in a few more minutes. The sociological changes in the American population after World War II with people moving much more frequently to different parts of the country meant that the old patterns of doing business based upon long-lasting relationships between the customer and the businessman were breaking down. Many of the "old-timers" who used to do their business downtown had died or moved, and new people moving into the area had no particular allegiance to the downtown area or relationships with the merchants. Patterns of friendship and shopping where people lived, worked, and shopped in the same place all their lives were gradually disappearing.

Even greater changes in these shopping patterns were to come with the invention of the personal computer and the creation of the World Wide Web on the Internet. Millions of Americans now do a significant portion of their shopping via their personal computer, laptop, or cell phone while traveling and being anywhere. It is the utmost in convenience. And for several generations of young people, "community" is now largely defined by who they friend on Internet modalities such as Facebook, My Space, and Twitter. Although it would be easy to be nostalgic and moan over the loss of the "good old days" as something that has been lost, other things have been gained. And I can only imagine that if Louis Spiegler were present in the digital age, with his progressive spirit and optimism, and fascination with modern technology (He had to own the first automobile in Des Plaines), he would fully embrace the digital technology and be selling everything from silk screen T-shirts to sandals on the Internet, with his trusted companion and advisor, Minnie, right by his side.

www.ingramcontent.com/pod-product-compliance
Lightning Source LLC
Chambersburg PA
CBHW081825290426

43661CB00125BA/884